MW00573815

# MAKING YOUR OWN
# REALITY

## ◆A SURVIVAL STORY◆

# MAKING YOUR OWN
# REALITY

◆ A SURVIVAL STORY ◆

## JAMES P. MEADE, JR., PH.D.

CITI OF
BOOKS

**CITIOFBOOKS, INC.**
3736 Eubank NE Suite A1
Albuquerque, NM 87111-3579
*www.citiofbooks.com*
Hotline:     1 (877) 389-2759
Fax:         1 (505) 930-7244

Ordering Information:

Quantity sales. Special discounts are available on quantity purchases by corporations, associations, and others. For details, contact the publisher at the address above.

Printed in the United States of America.

ISBN-13:    Softcover    978-1-959682-31-8
            eBook        978-1-959682-32-5
            Hardback     978-1-959682-33-2

Library of Congress Control Number: 2022920904

# Table of Contents

This book is dedicated to all the wonderful Miracle Workers who have always been there for me when I needed them most, especially my loving parents, James Meade, Sr. and Christine (Williams) Boyed, and my wonderful sister, Judi Lincoln, and my fantastic brothers, Leon "Squeak", David and Timothy Meade.

# Introducing Myself

SECOND CORINTHIANS 1:4

**B**efore she died of cancer, my previous wife, Marie-Louise, who earned her PhD in clinical psychology in 1980 four years before I did, and I would often discuss what might have caused me to evolve from snorting, growling, and grabbing at people to what I am today, which no one who sees me or meets me can even imagine. *Why me? I ask myself. Why am I so blessed?*

In 2 Corinthians 1:4, I feel that I am being told that God comforted me "in my tribulation" so I can help others who are suffering from their own tribulations. Of all the other reasons I have read or heard, this certainly makes the most sense. I am not singled out. God used many people to help me overcome my injuries—especially my parents and my siblings, Leon ("Squeak"), David, Judi, and Tim—and I feel an obligation to help others as a reason for my existence. A team around me was created to comfort and help people in need.

It is that simple, and nothing has been more important to me since the day I realized that I could have no better reason for being alive. In my heart, I know that God has blessed me more than I have the words to describe, and he continues to bless me every day of my life.

I

I am a firm believer that God has a plan for my life and all our lives. I do not pretend to know what God is or where God is, but I feel comfortable with the idea that every behavior has a consequence that is a response to a behavior, which in turn is a consequence of that response, which in turn ... and so on.

At the same time, I believe that God uses other people to guide us and help us be as perfect as we are willing to attempt to be. In the Bible, the disciple Matthew instructs us, "Be ye perfect as God is perfect," which I interpret to mean that I am to keep trying to be the best I can be.

This does not mean that I will ever be perfect, only that God is willing to be with me in all my efforts to better myself. No, I will never be perfect, but in my heart, I *know* that God will help me find whomever or whatever I will need to be as perfect as I can ever be, a better or more capable person than I am right now. When my efforts fall short of what they need to be, I am equally convinced in my heart that God will continue to help me until I reach the mark.

## JIM MEADE DIED, AND JAMES MEADE WAS BORN

Sometimes when I was scared, confused, and simply did not know how to move on, there were more people than I could count who were willing to offer me the unconditional kindness and guidance I needed, also fostering my determination to keep pushing on. Whatever the reality of God is, I feel that God directed these helpers.

I firmly believe that most of us have been blessed to meet people who always seem to be willing to help other people whenever they are asked or it becomes clear that their help is needed.

According to Richard Dawkins, "Miracles, by definition, violate the principles of science." Over the years, thousands of people have made a point to write to me, call me, or tell me in face-to-face meetings that I am a true miracle. This is humbling, and I think this is also an issue that deserves to be discussed.

I recently read an article in the Jehovah's Witness publication *The Watchtower*, which I feel I gain from reading, even if I am a devote Episcopalian/Catholic. The title of the article was "Miracles: Do They

Really Happen?" One section was "Common Objections Concerning Miracles."

The doctors who treated me after I crashed made it as obvious as they legally felt they could that I was either going to die or be a vegetable for the rest of my life. Obviously, my surviving after being struck in the head by the helicopter rotor blade that hit me so violently that it also knocked over my pilot's seat that was bolted to the floor seemed impossible. Thus we could say that James Meade died, and James Meade was born ten weeks later, a new life that had to learn everything that Jim Meade had learned in nineteen years.

Everyone I have ever talked to has told me that it was a "miracle" that I lived. I am fairly sure that some, maybe many, people are also convinced that the laws of nature must be responsible for my living as a functional human being. This theory does not have to disclaim the reality of God.

Whatever anyone chooses to believe can be both logically validated and disputed. More important is the reality that God uses other people to perform what we choose to call miracles, and these people are the miracle makers.

## MIRACLE WORKERS

The doctors who were responsible for me decided to have me transferred to the amputee ward so I could be with eighteen-, nineteen-, and twenty-year-old combat veterans who were continually active and had been brought to hospitals from battlefields via helicopters. Dr. Marx (not his real name) told my parents that the men in ward 13 would probably do more to help me want to live than he ever could do.

The men in ward 13 attempted to stimulate me to consciousness constantly during the week, and Kathy (my first wife), her mother, my parents, and my brothers and sister were with me every weekend. My doctors, nurses, and medics were there to help me twenty-four hours a day. My physical therapy nurse and ward nurse helped hold all the pieces of my hospital existence together.

This may sound somewhat strange, but I know that if I had been injured anywhere else, I probably would have died, for I know that God used these people to be there for me. My left leg and right foot were almost torn off, and my brain was scrambled. I started my new life in a body cast and could not see down the side of my bed. If it were not for all those miracle workers, I never would have found out that up was not down and that some people have legs. My life was my ward mates floating around the ward and landing on my bed without legs, and I could not see down to know that some people who came to my hospital bed actually had legs.

One of the significant symptoms of a traumatic brain injury is that the victim simply does not know what he does not know. I did not know that people had legs, because I had never seen legs, at least that I could remember, and I could not feel my own. I could not save myself, because I did not know *anything!*

I am not a miracle. It is the miracle workers God made who saved my life, and I have dedicated my life to being a miracle worker for other people whom God has chosen me to help in whatever way I possibly can.

In my heart, I know there are miracles, for I have met too many miracle workers to think otherwise. I am truly blessed that God has chosen to help me be the person I did not know how to become on my own.

## THREE TIMES IN LESS THAN THREE MONTHS

Some people might ask me how I know that God will help people in times of need. My answer always is that my faith is a product of what I have seen. I have had patients who have learned to do things that their doctors and other professionals concluded were nearly impossible, and I have seen miracles happen.

Throughout most of this book, I will use myself as an example. The reason for this is that I know exactly what I was feeling at the times I am describing, and I can never know exactly what somebody else is thinking or feeling. I hope this is helpful. Like any therapist, I use my experiences to help me recognize what might be good questions and appropriate statements.

There is something that I will repeat often, which I am confident is every bit as important as anything else I will discuss and equally as important as what I advise my patients to attempt. When I awakened from my ten-week coma (forty-five years ago), I did not know what parents were, and of course I had no idea who these people were who were kissing me and crying. With no memory of my past, I completely forgot the bonds that had once held us together.

Kathy and I had eloped to Idaho five days before my flight class flew to Vietnam (on a purple Braniff Airlines jet). Since we had never told anyone we were married, I called my parents on April 28, 1967, and broke the news to my father that I was married—and that my wife, is a senior in high school.

I also told him that I was in a hospital in Cu Chi after being shot down and wounded—shot down for the third time in two months. My father was quiet for a moment, and then he said in a calm voice, "You've got more gonads than I've got. After one time, I'd probably have turned in my papers." This is what he told me, but he proved different during his tours in Vietnam. He was in Vietnam for two years after my final crash and two years after my brother David was killed. A week later, I volunteered for a mission with my friend Billy Seale. I don't remember the call to my parents or ever eloping with Kathy. (She was a beautiful woman and person, but I felt that someone I did not know had me trapped, and our marriage ended in a friendly divorce.)

I gave her a gentle kiss on her cheek after the judge declared us divorced. I almost cried because I was completely alone, but at the same time, I knew that continuing to live with a stranger would drive me completely bonkers.

## THE PRODUCT OF EVERYTHING DONE

Every second of my existence has been more exciting than I have the words to describe, and I would not want to change a thing I have done or that has been done to me. Don't get me wrong. I have done things that have hurt people and wish I had never done, but at the same time, I realize that who I am today is a product of everything I have ever done. As long as I can learn from my behavior and can grow to be a person who gives to the world, I know I am a person of worth.

My faith in God is complete. This is despite the fact that I am a weak Christian and can be as selfish as the most selfish, self-centered person I have ever met. I have never had anyone try to kiss my ring, and no one has ever accused me of being perfect, nor has anyone thought about anointing me as a saint. Some people I know do not like me for valid reasons, even if they might only be valid to themselves. Whether they want to share their reasons or not, I do my best to represent my faith in God.

Still, I want to share something that I have only told a few people in the last forty-five years. I had my experience before I regained consciousness and told my father three or four years later. When I told my father, he cautioned me not to tell others, for they would think my story was due to my brain injury and would think I was crazy.

I did not want to have people think of me as being more mentally lacking than some people probably already did, so I kept what happened to me in my heart, with the exception of a few people I felt had open minds and who seemed to trust me as much as I trusted them.

When I tell someone that I know in my heart that there is a God, what I am doing is stressing my faith. To be honest, I don't know what or where God is, but in my heart, there is no doubt that something so much greater than I truly exists. What I experienced, more than simply saw, as part of my being was a brightness that I have never been able to describe. I felt this brightness as part of me and me as part of it.

I heard nothing. As readers may recall, I could not speak or understand the English language, but I could feel a message that was meant for me, and that message was part of the complete brightness.

I did not remember that I had been a helicopter pilot or that I had been in Vietnam. Still, the message of the warm brightness was that I would never be alone. Instantly, I knew that whatever was happening was *God* that simple. And I have never been alone except for those moments when I told myself I was alone and lonely, like anyone else.

My faith tells me that I do not have to be alone. My experience of the brightness was so complete that I feel I do not have to be without it, and God wants only the best for me. I feel secure that my welfare is important to God, and I have always known, as I make the effort to better myself, that God is with me. This gives me strength and determination when everything else tells me I want to quit; when I go on, I will not be alone.

# Chapter 1

## Some Information About Brain Injuries

### A MAN WHO KNOWS

As most people who know me will readily tell you, I feel I am just about the most blessed person on earth; give me a chance, and I will let you know too. In 1996, I had the honor of meeting psychologist and author Al Siebert, PhD, at a seminar. In 1997, he graciously signed a copy of his book *The Survivor Personality* for me. That book had impressed me more than almost any other book I had ever read.

Most books I have read that are not written by someone with a physical disability or a traumatic brain injury, regardless of the author's experience as a professional, suffer from an inability to relate what the individual feels or needs. Do not get me wrong; even with a PhD in psychology, I realize that I can never fully know what anyone else feels or experiences. On the other hand, I know what my feelings are or have been, and there is a chance that I may sometimes have a good idea of what my patients are feeling. In my copy of his book, Dr. Siebert inscribed, "For Jim—with much appreciation for a man who knows what this is all about! Al Siebert."

Even though I had earned my PhD thirteen years earlier, when he signed that book, I had to admit to him that relative to all there is to know, I did not know very much. Now, fifteen years after the inscription, I still have so much to learn. I feel so grateful that people I work with have been so patient as I have attempted to help them be the persons they want to be. They certainly helped *me,* and I thank them for their understanding that earning my PhD allowed me to work in this field; and what I learn comes from them.

## THE FOUR MAIN TYPES OF BRAIN INJURIES

I was nineteen years old when I graduated from army helicopter flight training, was commissioned a warrant officer, and received my orders for Vietnam—all on the same day. As you can understand, I was concerned about surviving, but I did not even begin to think that I might experience a brain injury. From what my family told me, a brain injury was something people simply did not get overly concerned thinking about.

As my parents learned in 1967, most doctors seemed to be fixated on the idea that individuals with brain injuries almost never got any better, and that there was not much they could do for the person except attempt to keep him comfortable and make him less of a burden on society. When I earned my PhD in 1984, our understanding of traumatic brain injuries (TBI) was not much better, and appropriate changes in TBI rehabilitation had not been made.

Lieutenant Karen Stevens, my physical therapist (PT) at Madigan General Hospital in Fort Lewis, Washington, was a caring and outstanding PT. Still, her work with me did not include techniques that would specifically benefit a brain-injured individual. As fantastic as she was to all of us who returned from Vietnam torn apart, all she could do was perform traditional physical therapy for battered bodies. Perhaps they treated me more delicately because I was more helpless than many of the other wounded soldiers at Madigan. But from what I have been told, nobody had any idea if treating me differently from patients who did not have brain injuries was appropriate or even necessary.

I might be safe to say that it was not until the 1990s that critical changes in the diagnosis of brain injuries occurred. It is interesting that intellectual papers became popular among academic communities, but new rehabilitation techniques were largely rejected due to their being of little help—if not completely worthless.

There are four primary types of brain injuries, and each explains the area of the brain injury and the effect the injury has on the body. On May 8, 1967, I experienced a TBI known as a *diffuse axonal injury* (DAI).

When the helicopter crashed into the jungle trees outside the fence around Tay Ninh, the main rotor blade broke off. Still spinning, it tore off the cockpit ceiling and was directly in line with my skull, above my eyes. The rotor blade struck me violently. My head hit the plate behind it, which was designed to shield me from shrapnel, with such force that my shielded seat, which was bolted to the cockpit floor, was knocked completely to the back of the helicopter—with me still in it.

Although I was an aircraft commander, this was my first flight since being shot down and wounded on April 27, and I was second in the pilot seat. I had volunteered to fly a combat mission with my Christian friend Billy Seale, who tells me I saved his life, because I took the brunt of the force from the rotor blade. If it had not hit me, it would have possibly cut off his head.

My skull was cut open like a cracked egg. Billy told me a couple of years ago that there was so much blood, he could not tell if I still had a face. Billy broke his leg in the crash, and I am so blessed that my friend did not have to suffer as I did. Billy is taller than I am, and he sat higher in his seat.

The DAI I experienced affects the entire brain. It occurs when the brain remains in motion inside the skull when the skull stops. In other words, the brain actually bounces inside the skull, and its nerve cells are pulled, stretched, and torn like elastic bands. According to John W. Cassidy, MD, "Since the forces involved also include rotation of the head around the neck, the entire brain is impacted by this diffuse form of trauma." The hallmark of DAI is immediate loss of consciousness.

I was unconscious for ten weeks, two weeks while returning to the United States and eight weeks at Madigan. My brain went "offline," and there was an immediate loss of memory that has never returned.

As when a plug is pulled on a computer, nothing that was written on the hard drive of the brain can ever be retrieved.

I had to relearn how to speak and understand English, walk, dress, feed myself, and most other things it takes to be a human being. But I did not retrieve a single memory of the first eighteen years of my life. I once faked a memory, and it did nothing to help my self-image.

Did you notice that I wrote the "first eighteen years of my life" rather than the first nineteen years? Jim Meade Jr. died in May 1967, and James Meade Jr. was born in July 1967. My memories of Jim are gone, but I am blessed. My family and friends have repeated my past so lovingly and so often that I claim those memories as my own. I don't remember the events but do remember being told about them many, many, many times.

In ward 13 at Madigan, my ward mates talked about the war so much that I feel I have mentally experienced a dozen years of constant combat. Pilots from Vietnam would stop and visit me. I was told several years later that my ward mates told my pilot friends that I "got it in the head," and they should tell me about all the heroic things I did. I could not speak very well then and do not remember most of what I was told. Sometimes I would act as if I remembered, but since I am such a poor liar, I pray that those people who know I was lying will forgive me. Living with a forgotten past can be so lonely, and I sometimes did not want to have to say, "No, I don't remember you."

I met a girl I had known for about three years before my brain injury. I tried hard to convince her that I remembered her because I really wanted to be friends with her again. But I ended up telling her so many fairy tales and agreeing with her so often about things she told me we had done in high school that she never called me back, even though I'd given her my address and phone number. She had obviously caught me and was not impressed. This was another loss in my life, and this time, it was entirely my fault. She seemed like such a nice person, and I hope she is happy.

Another major type of brain injury is *focal contusion injury*. This is a bruising of specific areas of the brain that is the "result of abrasion by the boney, roughened skull." Focal bruising occurs in specific areas of the brain rather than throughout the brain. Again, as written by

4

Cassidy, "The brain can be damaged at the point of direct contact as well as the opposite side of impact, or a coup-contrecoup injury, by the striking that occurs on the inside of the skull during the traumatic event."

*Focal hemorrhagic* or *ischemic injury* is common in strokes and TBIs. It is caused by the blockage or rupture of blood vessels that supply oxygen to areas of the brain. In other words, areas are damaged by the deprivation of blood and oxygen supply. Neurons (brain cells) cannot survive more than six or seven minutes without oxygenated blood. Depending on where the injury occurs, one person may lose the ability to talk and another may be unable to move a leg or an arm.

A fourth type of brain injury, a diffuse hypoxic or anoxic injury (DHAD), can be the most serious. It involves the loss of oxygen to the entire brain. For example, a person may experience a loss of oxygen due to a massive internal injury of the abdomen or other crucial organs, depriving oxygenated blood from getting to the heart and causing a heart attack. The most common cause of this type of brain injury is a massive heart attack that leads to a full-blown cardiopulmonary arrest. The victim can survive a cardiopulmonary arrest if cardiopulmonary resuscitation (CPR) is started soon enough. Even with survival, a brain injury can occur if the victim is deprived of oxygen for three to five minutes.

## DEGREES OF SEVERITY

We have looked at the types of brain injuries, but this is incomplete without categorizing them into their degrees of severity. While few people can name the types, at the same time, few people realize the degrees of brain injuries can be categorized as mild, moderate, severe, or catastrophic.

For some reason, different sources often seem to publicize different numbers regarding traumatic brain injuries, but we should be fairly safe if we state that between 1.6 and 1.7 million people in the United States have a traumatic brain injury every year, more than thirty times the number of people who die in auto accidents each year. After traumatic brain injuries, 80,000 to 100,000 people suffer long-term disabilities each year, and over 6.3 million American people live with TBI-caused disabilities. Men are about twice as likely as women to have TBIs.

## MILD

Of traumatic brain injuries, 70 to 80 percent are mild, and they are the most difficult to diagnose. At the same time, they have the best prognosis of all brain injuries, and individuals often recover fully in less than six months post-injury.

This can be good and bad. Just yesterday, I talked to a woman who said she had suffered a "little head injury" that "wasn't bad enough to go see a medical doctor," but on several occasions (more common lately), she has experienced times when she felt "woozy" or "out of it."

I told her I have worked with people who have suffered mild brain injuries for more than thirty-five years, and while her symptoms might mean little, I would recommend she visit her doctor and tell this to him. She responded with, "I do think they are associated, and I can't see wasting the money."

I have heard this so many times that it does not amaze me anymore. But at the same time, I have talked to victims of these mild injuries whose lives have been significantly disrupted by these symptoms that did not need to occur. I have seen these symptoms that began as mild annoyances end up changing lives—and not usually for the better. This does not have to happen; simply talking to a doctor can lead to fairly rapid remedies.

## MODERATE

A moderate brain injury's symptoms vary from person to person. No two brains are exactly alike, and it makes sense that no two brain injuries will be exactly alike. Some of these injuries may seem relatively minor, while some of these traumatic brain injuries can be somewhat confusing and complicated.

Some of the moderate TBI symptoms are lack of coordination, weakness, language difficulties, perception problems, memory problems, and planning and judgment problems. The injured person may be prevented from returning to work or school for up to several months, possibly longer.

## SEVERE

A severe brain injury is when the victim is comatose for more than one day. I was unconscious for a total of ten weeks and regained consciousness without the cognition or memory of anything I knew before the rotor blade struck me. The doctors told my family that even if I lived, they doubted I would ever be more than a vegetable.

My parents and Kathy were told that I probably would not be able to be independent even at the most basic level. Some people even with severe TBIs improve to the point that they can return to some work with reduced cognitive or physical challenges. The doctors surmised that I would not be one of this population.

I was not unconscious for one day. I was unconscious for seventy days and, after one year, my IQ test score was not even high enough to be the lowest IQ score that would keep me in the US army. I figured my flying days were over because I could not walk and do so many things that most human beings can do by the time they are in kindergarten.

Someone told my family that I might be transferred to a long-term facility (institution) that takes care of brain-injured people who cannot take care of themselves. As I recall I did not understand why they would do this to me. In my confused state, what I felt was fear that this would kill me, although I have no idea why I felt that way.

## CATASTROPHIC

According to John W Cassidy, MD, in his book, *Mind Storm*, "A brain injured person who remains unresponsive to the environment and requires total care for all his/her daily needs is considered to have suffered a catastrophic injury. They cannot speak, follow commands or even understand what is being said to them."

My parents knew that I was once considered by the doctors to be in a vegetative state. My mother was an extremely intelligent emergency room nurse, and she knew that my being institutionalized was not going to happen.

## MY THEORY

My theory is that my brain was so rattled by the main rotor blade that the neural pathways were completely disorganized, and the old messages that traveled from neuron to neuron ceased to exist. I have talked to neurologists and psychologists who, even if reluctantly, have told me that nothing else seems to make any sense.

I have never met or even heard of anyone else who might also be an example of this possibility. Still, I feel like a "work in progress," and the belief that I am not alone is very dear to me.

Some professionals have told me that this type of neuron compensation is unrealistic even to contemplate. All I am saying is that no other theory even begins to seem possible. I understand that the majority (about 80 percent) of brain injuries are mild, and that with appropriate care, they have extremely positive outcomes. Moderate to severe traumatic brain injuries may require years of rehabilitation therapies and immeasurable effort, and I pray that I am a realistic example that the brain can heal itself even after the most disabling experience.

My left leg is numb below my knee. I cannot smell or taste. I cannot run. I have come from an average of twenty grand mal seizures to six grand mal seizures a year. I can print fairly well, but writing in cursive frustrating. I cannot run even ten feet without throwing myself forward on my face. I cannot drive since my perception of curves no longer exists. The dexterity of my hands and feet is fairly pathetic. When I am tired, a spoon is more convenient than a fork. And sometimes when I least expect it, it is difficult for people to understand me.

I may have forgotten a couple of things. One reason is I that do not desire to dwell on all the things I cannot do. Not being stupid, I recognize my limitations. My parents and my brothers taught me that limitations are intended by God to let me know that there is more than one way to accomplish anything. I have had a fairly successful life, and I have loved every second of it, even the not- so-fun times.

## MOTHER

My mother once told me something that meant more to me than anything else I've ever been told. At times when my courage was lacking, this has given me strength I not only did not know I had but thought I did not have. It is so simple: "It is very difficult to complain about what you do not have or cannot do, when you are thanking God for all you do have and all you can do."

And I may have read this in a psychology book: Think positive and positive things happen; dwell on negative things and if positive things happen at all, they happen by accident, which is a pathetic way to live one's life.

# Chapter 2

## Introducing Myself

**M**ost people do not know this, and possibly don't care, but many motivational speakers and writers, certainly not all, have no more experience to give them any awareness of what they are speaking and writing about than being unemployed during some part of their lives. I might have entered this category except that I was determined to return to work, despite being rated 100 percent disabled by the Veterans Administration, and this took every bit of energy I could muster.

I have heard of a popular motivational speaker who choreographs every speech so that he accents the same words, is in the same places on the stage, and makes the same body movements during every word he speaks. He was an outstanding entertainer and made a great deal of money. He impressed the daylights out of me.

I do not begrudge him for his success. As I said, he was an entertainer, and the thousands of people who came to hear him were more than likely interested in a good show that would make them feel good.

If you read the *Reader's Digest* article before any other sections, you might become more than a bit confused. It must be obvious that it was not my idea to fly into the jungle trees, and I had nothing to do with surviving the rotor blade strike that caused me to be unconscious for ten weeks.

This is a history of how I was, written by the person I am now. My family tells me that I am completely different from the person I was before my experience, but my family has always been more important than anything else has, and my faith in the Supreme Being has always been the center of my life. I have never been able to recall the first eighteen years of my life, but over the years, I learned to love the people that I was told are my family, and everything I have experienced has caused me to feel that nothing less than a Perfect Being could have created the perfect objects that make up what we call "life."

It is important that readers sense that the tone of what I have written is not one of a community college lecturer or a university professor. My feelings and reactions are no different from many other people's experiences, and reading the book in the tone the reader feels I probably spoke in when I wrote them would probably make it easier to remember them.

Something that should be important to anyone who wants to change himself or herself for the better is that from the time I regained consciousness, I have been grateful for everything I have ever experienced. My mother, a faithful Christian, would tell me, "Be grateful for everything and you will be amazed how wonderful your life will be." I did not have to wait or hope that anything positive would happen. It simply did.

Every day for as long as I can remember, I have told myself that I am truly blessed, which has one benefit my mother never mentioned. Telling myself how blessed I am makes telling myself how lacking I am seem more than a little bit ridiculous. The two ideas simply do not go together.

Thinking or griping about the things we feel we deserve or need certainly does not cause anyone to feel better. But looking around and telling yourself how blessed you are puts you in a more positive mood. It merely seems to work that way.

## MY THREE WEEKS HOME

It was December 1965. It wasn't a cold day even for December, but the sky was gray and overcast, and the typical Oregon drizzle was as annoying as ever.

After saying good-bye to my good friends in the Delta Epsilon fraternity house at the University of Oregon, I grabbed my green suitcase and began walking toward Interstate 5, where I hoped it would not be too long before somebody would give me a ride from Eugene to Portland, where my family lived.

Standing with my leg against my suitcase next to the entrance to I-5 Northbound, memories of some of the great times at the University of Oregon rushed through my head so fast that I thought I was going to pass out. Still, I was not sad that I was leaving college. The last year and a half had been fantastic, but after growing up with a father who was in the army, moving on was an opportunity to create new memories and make new friends.

I was a little scared, yes. What would my new life be like? Some adjustments would surely be rougher than others. At the same time, I was convinced that there would also be some great times that I would never want to forget. For eighteen years, I had had no less than a great life. My family had lived in Banks, Oregon; Trieste, Italy; Fort Lewis and Seattle, Washington; West Point, New York; and Munich, Germany (where I went all four years to Munich American High School), and I was excited to experience what would happen next.

It had been over an hour, yet nobody had stopped to give me a ride to Portland. I had begun to wonder if I might have picked the wrong day to try to hitchhike home, but then a man stopped and asked me if I wanted a ride to Portland. As I clearly recall, I suddenly almost began to cry. For me, leaving Eugene and the U of O was the beginning of a new adventure. For months, all I had done was plan and dream of all these things that might or might not become reality, and getting into his car and leaving the University of Oregon was like stepping into a new world that was difficult for me to even imagine.

The very first thing the driver said to me after we got back on I-5 was that his son had won a gold medal in swimming at the 1964

Olympic Games. To say the least, I was more than a little bit impressed that he had bothered to stop and give me, a mere college student, a ride to Portland so I could spend three weeks visiting my family before joining the army. Of course, he did not know I was enlisting in the army in three weeks to go to basic training, helicopter flight training, and then (100 percent probably), Vietnam.

As far as he was concerned, I was probably another college student who was hitchhiking home. In fact, I don't think I told him more than I was a sophomore at the University of Oregon and was going home after completing fall term. He was obviously having a great time talking about his son, and I enjoyed listening to him.

My brother "Squeak" and I had been members of the Babe Ruth League in Munich and then were the European Champions in 1962, and I felt confident in assuming that my parents did not brag about us one bit less than he did about his son. (Still, I have often wondered if he ever read the article about me in the December 1970 *Reader's Digest* and had any idea that I was the student he drove from Eugene to Portland that misty morning in December 1965.

During the ride to Portland, I prayed that my parents would be proud of me for what I was doing. My father was a career command sergeant major in the army, and he made it obvious to me that he was super proud of me because I was in college. I had also been near the top of the freshman class academically and had been elected president of the U of O chapter of Phi Eta Sigma, the national freshman scholastic honor society. My father wanted me to become an army officer when I graduated in 1968.

I was only eighteen years old, and I was worried that my decisions to quit college, join the army, and go to war, hopefully as a helicopter pilot, wouldn't break my parents' hearts. My father and I hadn't gotten along very well, especially when I was in high school, but almost from the day I became a college student, we became the best of friends. In fact, I was not ashamed to tell people that my father was my best friend.

I was petrified that my decision to quit college would destroy the friendship that my father and I had worked so hard to develop. My father would drive down to Eugene from Portland at least once a month to visit me. He treated me with more respect than I thought was even possible. My father had always been my hero, even when I was a brat, and I needed his love and respect.

Still, in my heart, I felt that I knew what I had to do. It would have broken my heart if my decision hurt my parents, but my father had told me several years later that I told my parents, "I choose to be a helicopter pilot and go to Vietnam in order to *save* as many lives as I possibly can, and I'll be darned if any other mother's son is going to die in my place because I am too afraid to go. That just isn't going to happen." My father told me that he had never been prouder of anyone in his life or more scared.

When we got to Portland, it was still raining, and the driver drove me all the way to our home on Madison Street in southeast Portland. I had never before seen the man who drove me to Portland, and as pleasant a person as he seemed to be, I was not sure I wanted a stranger knowing where we lived. I told him I was anxious to begin this visit before joining the army and sincerely thanked him for making my day.

When we parked on the street in front of the living room window, I could see my mother vacuuming the living room rug. Of all the beautiful women I have met in my life, my mother, who was barely eighteen when I was born, was the most beautiful. She was wearing a scarf around her head and seemed to be wearing her gray bathrobe. As I got out of the car, I thanked the driver and asked him to tell

his son that I saw him on television. As I walked around the back of his car, he drove off, straight ahead and then left on Stark Street. It was raining harder than ever, but I wanted to watch my mother through the window. My little brother Tim was holding on to the end of the sofa and laughing with my mother about something.

It seemed like years since I had first decided to join the army and go to war about ten thousand miles away, and tears filled my eyes as I thought about how much I loved my family.

## THE MAN WHO FELL TO EARTH

Because of my injury, I cannot remember anything that happened before my eighteenth birthday. I would try to remember things, especially when people would say such things as, "James, you surely remember" Indeed, it sometimes made me feel less than human when

*Picture of Dr. James' brother, Squeak*

I had to face the fact that I have no past childhood beyond what I am told is my past. For much of my life, after being so badly injured in Vietnam, I felt like the man who came from nowhere!

I borrowed this belief from a movie I once saw (or a book I might have read), and I often feel like the man who fell to Earth. When I do, I feel super lonely. My life seems like a dream, and the only thing that makes any sense to me is that either I fell to earth or nothing I am experiencing is real. I was so lonely and could not think of any other reality except the emptiness that engulfed me the first years of this life, which began when I woke up in Madigan.

In my mind, I remembered what I wanted to be reality and felt that I had no choice but to create the best continuation of this reality that I possibly could. Indeed, the first few years were, at times, like living in a dream, sometimes a nightmare.

I like to think that I remember much of my entire freshman year at the University of Oregon, but at the same time, I know this can't be true, for I don't remember anyone I knew there, except Ed VanAlstyn, my English professor at the U of O and one of my favorite people in the world. As I pray I recall and have not merely created, Ed VanAlstyn was once a former Catholic priest and did his best to convince me not to join the army and go to war.

One hold I had on this possible reality of my past at the University of Oregon was a leather-bound copy of a book authored by Josefus about the time of Jesus Christ, but somehow my wife, Evelyn, or my sister, Judi, lost it. Nobody seemed to care that much that the book was so important to me. They didn't fully realize that that book could provide a grasp of reality. It was my only proof (to me) that these memories are actual realities. If I never find the book, then there is no proof that that part of my life existed.

It is strange how things that may seem so unimportant to other people can be so important in holding the reality of everything else together, and which, when absent from one's world, cause everything else to seem out of place and balance.

## WILMA

At the U of O, I was one of the nerds and apparently loved it. At least my memory indicates that I was having a good time. I was pledging at the Delta Epsilon fraternity, and was on the top of the world. I was a whiz kid, something I never expected after being a B student at the Munich American High School, where I was also senior class president and voted "male student with the best personality" all four years of high school, but I did not become excited about learning until college.

I apparently loved every second of campus life, especially the great conversations with people I no longer remember. My parents told me that in high school, the most important things in my life were God, Wilma Wright, books, and writing, but college was my environment, where I truly felt I belonged. This possibly will not sound strange to some college students, but every time I left the University of Oregon campus, I am told that I felt I was entering a different world.

Still, as much as I loved everything about the U of O, which I could hardly believe God had made part of my reality, I would read everything I could about the conflict in Vietnam, in which the United States was getting more and more involved. The more I read, the more convinced I became that as much as I loved college life, this was not where I belonged, not yet, not right then.

I would read articles about Special Forces advisors who were killed by Viet Cong or about war reporters such as Sean Flynn, Errol Flynn's son, being killed, and I would break into tears. Regardless of where I was at the time or whom I was with, I was not embarrassed. My age-mates were dying in a war about ten thousand miles away on another continent. As blessed as I felt being where I was, if I left to go fight a war for my country and returned alive, I wanted to return to college and even become a professor like my good friend Ed VanAlstyne.

But as much as I felt that I had no right to be in college while my peers were dying in our generation's war, and as loudly as I stressed that the United States was asked to protect South Vietnam from the Communist threat, which was also supposedly a threat to the United

States, I did not have the courage to just sign up and go. I had something to do first.

I knew I might die in Vietnam, and I needed to tell Wilma that I loved her one last time. So I flew back to Morristown, New Jersey, in the summer of 1965 to visit Wilma and her family. My plan was to tell Wilma that I was going to join the army, become a helicopter pilot like my cousin Jack Saint, and volunteer to go to Vietnam. In my mind, I was going to do the ageless manly thing: tell her I loved her but had to go to war, and it would be better for her if she loved someone other than a guy who might die in a war.

I must have heard the same script in at least a dozen World War II movies. The hero tells the woman he loves that he wants her to forget him and go on with her life without him because he is going off to war. In the next movie scene often, he dies gallantly, and tears run down her cheeks as she reads the letter that tells her that he was killed in combat. The last scene of the movie is fluffy clouds in an otherwise blue sky, with background music that almost every combat soldier dreams will be playing, when his loved ones are told that the soldier died gallantly in combat, a hero of heroes.

I could not even do that. Wilma was so beautiful, and even at eighteen years old, I loved her so much that I did not have the courage to tell her that I might not ever see her again. I did not have the guts to break her heart. Probably, just as truthfully, I think I knew in my heart that if she pleaded with me to change my mind, I might have done just that. I am no hero, but I also knew that I would regret it for the rest of my life if I allowed myself to be convinced that I had more important things to do. I left her without a hint of what I felt I had to do.

As the jet flew me up in the sky and home, I knew that I had done the right thing, but dear God, I hurt more than I thought was possible.

I probably stood in the front yard in the pouring rain and watched my mother through the window for about ten minute. The rain was coming down so hard that my mother didn't notice me at first through the raindrops that drenched the big living room window, and I did not even consider going in right away. I was dreaming and crying … just standing there. The rain was pouring down my face as I watched my mother do what I had seen her do so many times.

My Birthday is May 8, 1946
So.... on May 8, 1967. I
turned 21, was with Bill
ant my drunken Mother, received
diamond earrings — CAN'T
BELIEVE How Ym Spent your
Day! Oh, My!

*Picture of Wilma with a note to James about
her birthday on May 8, 1967.*

19

When my mother noticed me, she smiled at me and lifted the scarf away from her face. She was happy to see me and waved at me to come inside the house and out of the rain. My mother's broad smile quickly changed to an expression of absolute terror and shock. She started crying, and I could read her lips as she looked to the sky and started yelling, "No, no, no, no, God, no!" Tim, who had no idea what was going on, also began crying.

It had struck her that my final exams were not scheduled to end for another week, and it instantly became obvious to her that I had done what she had always feared: I had quit college and joined the army, which meant to her, without any doubt, that I would be going to Vietnam.

My parents knew I had already passed all the tests to be accepted to attend flight training to become a helicopter pilot. I was only eighteen years old, a sophomore in college, and still my mother's "oldest baby." To her, I had no business going in the army and to war, and when reality struck her, it almost destroyed her world.

I feel fairly sure I must be exaggerating, but in my mind, my mother kept crying and screaming for the next three weeks until December 27, the day I caught a bus at the Greyhound bus station in downtown Portland. Along with about thirty other inductees, we would travel to the Portland International Airport and get on a jet to Fort Polk, Louisiana, home of those bound for Vietnam.

When he came home, my father told my mother that her crying and screaming probably would only cause me to be more scared than he was sure I already was, but again, my mother was only eighteen when I was born, and in a way, we grew up together. When my mother hurt, I hurt, and when I hurt or was scared, my mother sensed my emotions without my having to tell her a thing. To be truthful, I cannot remember a time in my entire life when she could not, as they say, read me like a book.

Whenever my mother yelled, I knew that something was not right, and this time, something was not right with her heart. She was scared because she knew she would not be able to protect me if I was hurt, not this time. In seventeen months, she would save my life, but now it was my turn to help her. She had raised me for eighteen years, and it was my turn to help her let go, at least enough for me to become my own person.

## BEING HOME

In seventeen months, I would be flown back from Vietnam more dead than alive. When I neared death even more a few days later, my mother would beg the doctor to try something new. Just watching me and waiting for some sign of improvement did not make any sense at all to her. One time my mother, an emergency room nurse, flat out prevented an army nurse from giving me a certain medication because she knew it would kill me. I was unconscious for ten weeks, and for four of those ten weeks, she and Kathy never left me. My mother is still my mother, and yes, I am still her "little boy." I am okay with that. It even feels good.

When I was sixty-three years old, a doctor at the VA told Evelyn and me that I am apparently still dying.

My mother telephoned my father and immediately told him that I had come home. My father told me she was hysterical. Like so many mothers at the time, she *knew* I was joining the army, and she *knew* this meant I would be going to Vietnam. My father was less emotional because we had discussed my feelings about how my being in college while other Americans my age were fighting for their lives did not seem right to me. He knew it was just a matter of time. I had made my feelings obvious to him and, as his father had done for him in World War II, there was not a second that he did not support me.

My father told me at the Greyhound station before I was taken to the airport that hearing my mother tell him I had quit college to join the army and, yes, go to Vietnam was like getting punched in the stomach, but he knew this was something I felt I had to do. With tears in his eyes, he added that he was scared for me, as any sane father would be, if I joined the army while the country was at war. With tight lips, he told me that he was prouder of me than I could ever imagine.

For the next three weeks after I came home, my parents took off as much time from work as they possibly could, and it was a great three weeks. Squeak was a senior and David a junior at David Douglas High

School. Judi was in seventh grade, and Tim was not yet in school. The family did as many things together as we possibly could.

One thing my mother could never forget, as my father repeated it almost daily, was that in a year, if I completed flight school (of which he had no doubts), I would be commissioned a warrant officer and given flight wings as an army helicopter pilot—and I would only be nineteen years old. My father told me several years later that he had to keep repeating that I would be a nineteen-year-old officer and pilot to keep from crying like a baby.

At a time when I needed my family's support more than I ever had, my parents, brothers, and sister told me repeatedly how proud of me they were and how much they loved me. Tim, who was four, told me that he loved me and was proud of me, as much as anybody else in the family. I am not sure he even knew what going to war meant.

Those three weeks were so wonderful that they seemed to pass by in a few days rather than weeks. I never told them, but I needed their open love and support more than anything in the world because, as successfully as I had hidden my feelings, although not as terrified as my mother was, I was really scared. My fraternity house study room walls had been almost entirely covered with pictures of dead or dying soldiers and journalists, and I could just imagine my picture ending up on someone's wall too.

Actually, being shot down and killed in Vietnam was not my main worry. In Germany, where I went to high school, a person could not get a driver's license until he was eighteen years old. I was a sixteen-year-old senior in high school and obviously did not have a driver's license. During my first year of college, I did not have a driver's license. As a matter of fact, and this is the honest truth, in college I would ask girls out on dates and ask them what time they were going to pick *me* up!

In June 1965, my father taught me to drive and bought me a 1959 Renault Dalphine so I could get to work at a paper company in north Portland. In August 1965, I totaled it while driving home from work at about one in the morning.

Flying a helicopter seemed like a completely different world to me. The army recruiter had already told me that the chances were 100 percent that I would be sent to Vietnam, which to say the least, was the least of my worries. What actually scared me was the thought that I would not complete flight school and would have to tell my family. They were so proud of me, and the last thing I wanted to do was disappoint them.

## MY LITTLE BROTHER DAVID

My little brother David joined the army after I was transferred to the Veterans Administration Hospital in Portland, Oregon. He wanted to be an officer and a pilot like his big brother, but he was unable to pass the eye examination, which required twenty- twenty vision. So after basic training, jump school, officers candidate school and Special Forces training, he was commissioned a second lieutenant, his dream!

In his Green Beret uniform and combat boots, he looked ten feet tall. We had done pretty much the same things all our lives, and it made me so proud when he wrote on his OCS picture that he wanted to be an officer just like me.

On May 15, 1970, three years and one week after my helicopter crash, David was killed in Vietnam. He was twenty-one years old. I think of David every single day and miss him much more that I have words to express. The most special day in my life was the day I was the best man at his and Sally's wedding.

I love all my brothers and my sister, and David and I were best friends as well. Our love for David bonded the love the rest of us have for each other.

My mother has blamed my father for as long as I can remember for David and me choosing to join the army and go to war. She always seemed to need to believe that the true reason I volunteered to be a helicopter pilot to fly into combat was to make my father proud of me. The same goes for David. She blamed my father when she divorced him, and she still does.

My mother has never been willing to accept that I did not need to join the army and go to war to gain my father's respect. He was so proud of me for going to college. He told me every time I called home and every time he came to visit me in Eugene. Honestly, I was afraid he would be mad at me and call me a quitter for leaving college.

*Picture of Dr. James' brother, Lt. David E. Meade in his uniform.*

My acceptance into helicopter flight school also caused my father to be proud of me, but he told me once, and never brought it up again that he would have been just as proud of me if I had stayed home and finished college. He prayed that I would return to college after my tour of duty in the army. He supported me and, much like a friend, simply told me, "If you are man enough to make this decision, I am man enough to support you one hundred percent."

## THE GREYHOUND BUS STATION

The three-week visit with my family before I joined the army went by so quickly, and I cannot remember anything clearly in particular. We went to a Blazer basketball game and visited my grandparents a couple of times. I spent a lot of time having fun and laughing with Squeak and David. What I remember most fondly was the time we spent eating meals as a family, laughing and solving all the world's problems. Our time together was so great!

One event that I feel I have a clear memory of means more to me than I could ever fully describe. When I kissed my mother good-bye, she of course, became frantic again. To my mother, her children have always been the most important things in the universe, and it was obvious she did not want to let me go. (Even after over forty years, I can still see the tears that streamed down her face, and even now as I write this, it brings tears to my eyes and I cry as well.)

As we left home, my father was cool and calm. He was so calm and reserved that I wondered if he might be trying to prepare me for the indifferent and belligerent drill sergeants (DIs) that I expected would be in my face upon my arrival at Fort Polk.

My father, a soldier's soldier who loved everything about the army, was dressed in his always professionally laundered ribbon- checked green dress uniform and wore his perfectly polished black shoes that almost reflected his face when he looked down at them. He was the second or third soldier in the army to be promoted to the rank of command sergeant major E9, and he was the proudest soldier I have ever met.

When we arrived at the Greyhound bus station, my father did something that caught me completely by surprise. Before we got out of the car, he took his jacket off, put it in the backseat, and turned his green dress uniform cap around on his head. Then he turned to me and with tears in his eyes said, "If anybody sees a sergeant major crying in there because his son is going into the army, it will probably scare the living daylights out of a lot of recruits and their parents."

Tears also began to come to my eyes, but as my father hugged me, he continued, "I don't think my disguise is as good as I had hoped. I see two dads and half a dozen recruits wetting their pants." We both burst out laughing, and we laughed some more, nearly unable to stop. I wrote to Squeak in 1967 and told him what I said: "Dad, the crease in your green dress trousers would slice butter—what do you expect?'"

We continued laughing so hard that we could hardly walk. He was the father, I was the son, and during this most important time in our lives together, we were having fun.

When he said "I love you, son" when I had to leave, with tears gently flowing down his smiling face, I was never more sure that my father loved me. My family's love and support did not take away the fear, but it made me certain that everything was going to be just fine. The most important people in my world loved me completely, which made facing *anything* that much more doable.

## THE REAL BATTLE

Something we were told in the first preflight class is not only the first thing I wrote home about being in flight school, but it is also the first thing I was told about helicopters, period. They may have told it to new flight school students who were too scared to do everything they had to do to become army pilots: "Drop out now and don't think you still have time to quit after you are dead." It was probably also meant to convince students that flying helicopters into combat would be the most dangerous thing they would ever do in their entire lives.

I have read several articles in which flying helicopters in combat was called the most dangerous job in the history of warfare, and it was surely that. What the instructor pilot told us would probably cause anyone to rethink whether he actually wants to be a helicopter pilot at least one more time, maybe two. My flight classmates were probably attracted by the adventure of flying helicopters, especially into combat.

My friend Guy Nelson was the youngest member of the class and the first to die. Jerry McKenzie was one of the youngest and the last to die in Vietnam.

Despite this potential excitement, we were all hoping that the helicopter would not be fighting us, and when the instructor pilot told us, "Helicopters are not meant to fly; indeed, aerodynamically, helicopters are not supposed to be able to fly at all," you can bet that for many students, the pucker factor became a distinct issue. For the couple of students who never attended another class, that was possibly the smartest thing they ever did.

For some of the rest of us, the excitement of the new adventure easily quintupled. I became so excited that I thought I was going to wet my fatigue pants. (In Vietnam, I can remember several air assaults when the tracer bullets started hitting my helicopter. I could hear the *ping, ping, ping* as bullets hit, and I wet my pants—just let 'er rip like a little kid.)

*Picture of Command Sergeant Major James P.
Meade, Sr., Dr. James Meade's father.*

**TELEGRAM**

843P PDT MAY 9 67 LLA550
SYA562 SY WA005 XV GOVT PD 4 EXTRA FAX WASHINGTON DC 9 1045P
EDT
MR AND MRS JAMES P MEADE, DONT PHONE, REPORT DELIVERY
  14009 SOUTHEAST MADISON PORTLAND ORG
THE SECRETARY OF THE ARMY HAS ASKED ME TO EXPRESS HIS DEEP
REGRET THAT YOUR SON WARRANT OFFICER JAMES P. MEADE JR. WAS
PLACED ON THE SERIOUSLY ILL LIST IN VIETNAM ON 8 MAY 1967
AS THE RESULT OF FRACTURED SKULL. HE WAS PILOT ON UH-1B HELICOPTER
RETURNING FROM A COMBAT OPERATION WHEN AIRCRAFT CRASHED. IN
THE JUDGMENT OF THE ATTENDING PHYSICIAN, HIS CONDITION IS OF
SUCH SEVERITY THAT THERE IS CAUSE FOR CONCERN, BUT NO IMMINENT
DANGER TO LIFE. PLEASE BE ASSURED THAT THE BEST MEDICAL FACILITIES
AND DOCTORS HAVE BEEN MADE AVAILABLE AND EVERY MEASURE IS BEING
TAKEN TO AID HIM. A REPORT OF HIS PROGRESS WILL BE FURNISHED
YOU IN ABOUT FIVE DAYS. IF THERE IS ANY CHANGE IN HIS CONDITION

# WESTERN UNION
**TELEGRAM**

SY WA005 2

YOU WILL BE ADVISED IMMEDIATELY. ADDRESS MAIL TO HIM AT 24TH
EVACUATION HOSPITAL APO SAN FRANCISCO 96491
  KENNETH G WICKHAM GENERAL USA F21 & 22 THE ADJUTANT GENERAL
EYLM

# WESTERN UNION
**TELEGRAM**

955A PDT MAY 14 67 LLA282
SYA106 SY WA455 XV GOVT PD 3 EXTRA FAX WASHINGTON DC 14 1230P
EDT
MRS KATHLEEN L MEADE, DONT PHONE
  4416 SOUTHEAST 113 PORTLAND ORG
ADDITIONAL INFORMATION RECEIVED STATES THAT THE CONDITION OF
YOUR HUSBAND, WARRANT OFFICER JAMES P. MEADE JR. REMAINS THE
SAME. HE IS STILL SERIOUSLY ILL. PERIOD
OF HOSPITALIZATION IS UNDETERMINED. EVACUATION TO THE UNITED
STATES IS NOT CONTEMPLATED AT THIS TIME.
YOU WILL BE PROMPTLY ADVISED AS ADDITIONAL INFORMATION IS RECEIVED
  KENNETH G WICHAM MAJOR GENERAL USA THE ADJUTANT GENERAL
(48).

*Western telegram on May 9 and May 14, 1967.*

To anyone who knows my story, it must be obvious that my real war was not in Vietnam. My real war was surviving my wounds and attempting to recover a semblance of humanness that would enable me to be, and more importantly to feel, accepted by a society that I could no longer remember and did not even recognize.

Like so many of the other physically or mentally limited, especially the brain-injured people I have met and worked with over the years, I felt so lonely and completely alone. There was nothing more important to me in the entire universe than being accepted. I will repeat this throughout this book because the importance of being accepted and feeling this acceptance (remember this) is as important as anything else you will learn from this book or any similar book you will ever read.

I will also discuss my efforts to rehabilitate myself. No one can rehabilitate anyone else; in reality, only you can rehabilitate yourself. Many well-intending professionals claim that they can, but all anyone else can do is present the tools that may or may not be right for the disabled person.

I have a PhD in clinical psychology. I had to work hard for my degrees, and I am very proud of them. I have a bachelor of science in psychology from Portland State University, a master of arts in counseling from Fresno State University, and a PhD in psychology from International College. The primary thing I have learned even after earning all these academic credentials is that there is so very much to learn that in some ways, I am downright ignorant.

## JEANINE

New theories replace theories about just about anything on a constant basis. When I was brain injured forty-five years ago, medical professionals were confident in saying that there was no chance I would survive my injury and, to protect themselves if I did survive, they said that there was almost no chance I would ever be more than the equivalent of a vegetable. Apparently, the only people who believed I would not only survive my wounds but also overcome how severely my body had been torn apart were my parents and my siblings.

It might seem strange to some people that of all the experiences I have had in the last forty-five years, since my helicopter crashed and my brain was battered by the rotor blade of my helicopter, the ones I remember best are the ones when people told me that I would not be able to accomplish some goal, for they thought I no longer had the mental ability to do so. In other words, those people, without question, accepted what they were told.

I doubt that he meant what his words seemed to express, but the afternoon my stepfather told me that I should quit college and get a job because I was brain injured and not capable of being smart enough to get a college degree, I wanted to die. His words caused me to feel completely worthless. I felt unacceptable, that I had no value whatsoever.

If I had actually been an honor student and the president of Phi Eta Sigma at the University of Oregon in 1964 and 1965, I was confused. My blood father had told me that if I was willing to do whatever it took to accomplish my goals, I would be successful, and I knew I was willing to do whatever it took to graduate from college. I could not even respond to my stepfather. All I could do was sit there. I hurt so much that I could not even cry. I was in shock.

I wanted to scream to my father to tell my stepfather that he was wrong, but my father was in Vietnam. David was in the army in Special Forces training, and Squeak was at Pacific University in Forest Grove, Oregon. I felt completely alone. Like a desperate and confused child, I needed someone to hold me and tell me that I was not hopelessly stupid, that I did have value and that I was not bad.

I remember praying one day that Jeanine, my mother-in-law, was home. For some reason, I felt my first wife, Kathy, was ashamed of me and did not even like me. For that and other reasons, I did not want to share with Kathy (or my mother) what my stepfather said to me. It did not help that for some reason, I felt ashamed of myself).

Jeanine was kinder to me than anyone else I knew, and she lovingly told me, "Your stepfather is wrong. He is wrong, and someday you are going to show him just how wrong he is." Jeanine was my true friend and a truly beautiful person. I never stopped loving her, even after being divorced from her daughter for over three decades.

## TOOLS

Jeanine, thank you I feel I showed him that I am not stupid but also that some things are important to me, even if they are not important to anyone else. I am willing to do whatever I have to do, like study every chance I can.

I think I did something so much more important than proving something to someone else when I was willing to do everything that I needed to do to finish college. External factors usually seem to be our primary motivators, and this can be important, but what I actually did was prove to *myself* that I could accomplish anything if I was willing to do what it takes to accomplish my goals.

It's this simple: The more things I accomplished, the more things I wanted to accomplish. That may sound simplistic, almost to the point of sounding idiotic, if not a bit trite. But the truth is that it does not take big intellectual words to make something true. In case you did not know this, most new ideas, even ones that change the way we live our lives, are not the products of the efforts of well-known people who have written books or who have college degrees or done other outstanding things.

Dreams do not simply come true. Things that we want to happen do so because we do what it takes to make them happen. That said, even with all the effort, support, and encouragement in the world—and the best self-image in town—without the tools to be successful, all a person can hope for is a frustrating life, spinning his wheels. I think I can safely say that I have accomplished a fair amount in my life since Vietnam and waking up to a new life, but *please* do not doubt for a single second that I have also spent a lot of my time spinning my wheels without going anywhere.

Indeed, I am often congratulated for not giving up and quitting. I will be truthful and admit that this is great for my ego, and the positive comments are great motivators, but I must also confess that I am the king of quitters. I have easily quit hundreds of times more often than I have completed projects, even projects I began with the greatest of intentions. I look back and tell myself that I wish I had completed some of those projects. Isn't it fun telling ourselves, "Boy, oh boy, that is an idea that sure would have made me rich and famous, if I had tried just a little bit harder." I know these thoughts usually have no basis in reality, but again, it sure can be fun, can't it?

On the other hand, what is wrong with changing one's mind? My sister-in-law, Gail and I were discussing this about twenty years ago. She was a therapist before she retired, and in her usual straightforward manner, she said, "What on earth is wrong with deciding, *Hey, I don't want to continue in the direction I am going, because I don't think the route I am taking to try to achieve my goal is the best one for me?*" Does not following the same path all your life make you a failure? There's nothing wrong with thinking, *I'm not going to be able to accomplish my goal if I keep trying to do it the way I am, and darn it, I'm going to change my approach.* As long as one does not decide to do absolutely nothing, there is nothing wrong with changing direction. Despite this conclusion, however, there are some things that I must always consider whenever I dream or plan how I hope to accomplish anything.

We might want to get into this more later in another book but remember, I am disabled. I have physical limitations that prevent me from doing some things I used to be able to do, things that many people take for granted. I cannot run even a few yards; my fine motor dexterity is definitely lacking. I cannot smell or taste, I cannot talk clearly when I am tired, and my posttraumatic seizures (epilepsy) prevent me from driving and skydiving. I certainly don't have the energy or balance I wish I had. I could go on and on, but the point I want to make is that I have some physical limitations that I consider real bummers.

I love being with my wife, my brothers and their wives, and my sister more than anything else. On New Year's Eve a year or two ago, I tried to stay up until midnight in spite of being exhausted and knowing that staying up late is not good for me and causes me to be almost worthless for the next couple of days. I did a dumb thing. I knew my limitations and chose to ignore them. To pay for ignorance and attempting to seem able-bodied, I had a grand mal seizure.

Living with my limitations is not always fun, and on this occasion, I would have been so much smarter to simply have gone to bed. Did I impress anyone because I ignored those signs that told me I should have wished everyone happy New Year at ten o'clock and gotten the sleep I needed? I don't think so. I don't know whom I was trying to impress, but it didn't work.

Despite the errors I still make, possibly every day, I have learned a lot about being disabled over the last decades, which has made my life so much easier and much more fun than many people could ever imagine. Maybe I would have learned some of these things by putting two and two together and hopefully coming close to four. Also, my wife, who is Japanese and from Hawaii, is a nurse and my eternal companion, and she has truly blessed me by being part of my life. She has helped me learn so much and enjoy every second of the journey.

I am also grateful to the disabled people I have counseled around the United States and the world who have shared with me how they have learned to overcome their limitations and their mistakes, and how they have been able to make their own realities. I have been blessed that people have invited me into their lives and allowed me the honor of helping them create realities that we learned together. You already know that I have a PhD in psychology, and obviously,

I have read more than a few books, listened to *many* lectures, and been a part of some great discussions that were mind-boggling and exciting. I have loved being a mental health counselor, and learning my trade has been a source of happiness that I doubt I could ever fully describe. At the same time, the people I have worked with have taught me more than I could ever learn in books.

When I discuss how I have learned to overcome many of my limitations, what I am actually doing is sharing what I have learned from some very special people.

## THE PEOPLE

My father taught me the most important tool in learning to overcome my limitations, and I use that same tool to help individuals I feel will benefit the most from it. He was one of the smartest men I have ever met, although he quit Banks High School in Oregon during his third effort to pass his sophomore year. Actually, he did not fail his classes three years in a row. He pulled some prank on another student, and when he was sent to the principal's office, my father told the principal that he did not have to send him home ... because he quit!

Ed VanAllstyne is the most intelligent scholar I have ever met; my mother is the greatest mother I could ever have; Marie-Louise deBronac, PhD, is the most intelligent woman I have ever had the honor of knowing; Wilma Wright is the most beautiful woman and person I have ever known, Sergeant Roberts is probably the best drill sergeant the army has ever had; and to top it off, my father was the most intelligent person I ever knew. Some of my opinions change rather often, but these opinions are firm.

Everyone on Earth has worth or value in the eyes of God, and these people I have mentioned have special meaning to me. My parents, more than anyone else, had the ability to guide me in forming the humanness I would use to create the personality and skills that would distinguish me from 150 pounds of dough.

My father could not recall where he learned the skills he taught me. As far as he was concerned, he taught me things that always seemed natural to him. They definitely weren't learned in high school. He told me that if he learned them anywhere, it had to be the army. (How did I guess he would say that?)

My ward mates in ward 13, the amputee ward at Madigan General Hospital, took wonderful care of me as if I were a little brother, even though I was a warrant officer and the only officer in the ward. Second to my mother and Kathy, my ward mates were the ones who saved my life. The doctors and nurses kept my body in some semblance of a stable condition, but it was my ward mates, the nurses, and the orderlies who helped me create a desire to live. I was at Madigan for almost a year and a half before I was transferred to the old VA Hospital in Portland, Oregon, and they became my family, my pseudo-parents.

As far as I am concerned, there is no doubt that the most powerful tool there is in saving a life is the expressed love of husbands, wives, parents, siblings, children, or other loved ones. There does not seem to be scientific research to explain the power of love or why there are times when not all the love in the world can save a life. Still, I have repeatedly seen how the motivation, and the support of love make the difference between life and death and the possibility of complete rehabilitation. My first wife, Kathy, and my mother stayed with me my first thirty days at Madigan General Hospital, and in my heart, I have no doubt that it was their demonstrations of love that saved my life. The doctors and nurses did an outstanding job of helping them.

## THE RUBBER BALL

The first time I can remember my father working with me was also the first time, as I recall, that my doctors allowed my parents to bring me home on a convalescent leave. The doctors at Madigan could only do so much. The hospital's wards were full of soldiers who had been so seriously wounded that they had to be brought to hospitals in the United States. And as with many other wounded soldiers, the doctors felt that my parents and family could do more for me than they could.

I believe that the first exercise my father had me do was sit on the floor in the hallway, with my back against the wall and pillows all around me to hold me in a sitting position. My father then told me that he would roll a medium-sized rubber ball to me, and when the ball reached me (after rolling about five feet), I was to stop the ball and roll it back to him. I remember being able to sense his excitement, while my mother has told me that she could also see the fear in his eyes.

He would roll the rubber ball to me, expecting and hoping that I would be able to stop it and roll it back to him. I was then twenty, and my father told me that he had prayed to God to be with me because, like my doctor at Madigan, he did not know what to do next if I were unable to do this exercise. He told me years later that he had played this same game with me when I was a baby.

My father would smile broadly and say, "Here it comes." He'd roll a ball the size of a beach ball toward me, wanting me to stop the ball with my hands and roll it back to him without needing to exert much more than a minimum amount of energy, as any one-year-old could do.

The ball rolled approximately five feet to me and bounced off my chest. I fell forward on the floor as I tried to catch it. I was not blind and saw the ball, but my brain could not understand the message from my eyes that the ball was actually rolling toward me.

My brother Squeak told me that my father was so great. He was crying, and tears were rushing from his eyes as he struggled to smile. "Okay, Jim, you missed that one," he told me. "We'll try again. Just relax a minute first. Maybe you weren't ready when I rolled the last ball. Tell me when you are ready. That one was my fault. Just relax and you will do great."

My father rolled the ball to me repeatedly. And over and over again, the ball would bounce off my chest. I would reach for the ball as it rolled away from me, falling on my face, and the ball would roll back to my father. I did not know that I was not stopping the ball.

Even after all this time, it still brings tears to my eyes when I think about the tears on my father's cheeks as he told me I was doing great and would do even better the next time. I could not understand at the time why my father was crying. He was also smiling, which would have been a mixed message to the average person. All I knew was that he was there for me, and I looked forward to the next time we played with the ball.

It was not until years later that my father told me how scared he was for me. Due to the extent of my brain injury, my brain, at that time, could not react fast enough to instruct me to stop the ball that my father rolled to me and roll it back to him.

I could not walk, feed, or dress myself—or do almost anything I had been able to do before the crash—and my father was noticing that I had limitations from my brain injury that might never improve. I was the oldest son, and my father told me that he was in more pain than he ever thought anybody could survive. During one of our talks, he told me that he was scared to death and knew that if I died, he would die right next to me.

My father said that it was obvious to him that I needed to relearn how to be a human being again. And it was apparent to everyone that I knew less now than when I was a young child. My parents discussed my condition for hours at a time. As hard as he tried, he could not fathom anything that would help rebuild my damaged brain.

My mother was the nurse while, as far as he was concerned, he was just a soldier, and all this "medical stuff" made him feel stupid. What could *he* do that the doctors did not know and probably had already attempted? He told me that he remembered thinking, *Dear God, I did not even finish high school. What the heck do I know?*

What he did know was that he taught many soldiers to be the professionals that no one else believed they could ever become, and he was proud of helping the young children he had coached become champion athletes. He had coached the Little League basketball team that my brothers and I were on at West Point, which won the league championship. He also coached our Little League baseball team and guided my brother Squeak to become a member of the US all-star Little League baseball team. Squeak was a champion athlete in both high school track and basketball and attended Pacific University all four years on a baseball scholarship.

In 1960, I was chosen the outstanding pre–high school dependent at West Point, where my father was the sergeant major of the Corps of Cadets.

My father used the same skills to coach other coaches and team members of our Babe Ruth baseball team in Munich, Germany, in 1962. We then went on to became the Munich champions, then the Germany Champions, and then the European Babe Ruth champions. We would have gone back to the United States to play in the Babe Ruth World Series, but neither the army nor the air force in Europe had the funds to send our team to play in the United States. I have met many people over the years who were convinced that our team could have won that too.

In Vietnam, he was a command sergeant major of the Americal Division, the largest army division in the world at that time, and what he taught other people, he practiced every day. My father had no idea that what he merely called "natural" was called "imagery" by psychologists. All the theories that I read to him about imagery years later were, to him, no more than intellectual harangue that he did not even attempt to understand. I really feel that he was smarter than he gave himself credit for. Most intellectual minds that have attempted to explain imagery to each other do so in jargon only they can understand.

What my father did know was that practicing an activity in your mind could be as useful as practicing the same activity in physical reality. Something I added later, after teaching this tool several times, was that the mental image had to be formed correctly. To accomplish that required repetitive practice in the mind until one felt comfortable enough to practice the exercise in physical reality.

Some people have difficulty forming a particular image and need to practice forming some images of an activity more than others do. This seems to be especially true for people with serious brain injuries. Like other rehabilitation techniques, the use of imagery does not seem appropriate for everyone.

Any working brain is constantly rebuilding itself from day one of life. As the person experiences new stimulations, new neurons and synapses are created and new neuron patterns are formed. The original idea that one is born with a brain that never changes was probably thought up by accepted intellectuals and experts based on the time in history and amount of knowledge that existed. These were the most powerful people at the time, and society determined that they must be correct; questioning was looked upon as unintelligent. This has probably been an unpleasant fact since the existence of the first three-person group.

## TAKING IT BACK

When I received my bachelor's degree, my father and my first son, James, came to the graduation ceremony, and I told my father, "After I receive my diploma, we've got to get out of here fast, because when they discover that I don't know anything, they're going to take it back." Eight years later, when I received my master's degree, I told my family the same thing. In 1984, my proud parents flew from Portland to Sacramento when I was awarded my doctorate of philosophy in psychology. And yes, I told them the same thing yet again.

It amazes me! There is so much to know. How can people study for even a hundred-plus years and think they have possibly put even a dent into all there is to know about *anything*?

Again, have you ever noticed how fast theories are replaced with "new" theories that often debunk the old theories and make it seem as if only an idiot could have believed the "old" theory? We should consider so much for the concept of discovering the "final" answer to anything. Nothing stays constant, even the perception of the meaning.

The other day, I was walking through the Barnes & Noble bookstore, and as usual, I was skimming through the new books about the brain. In a seemingly well-researched and well-written book by Patt Lind-Kyle, I read this: "It has only been since 1998 that scientists have discovered that you can teach an old dog new tricks." What she was referencing is the new research that has revealed that the brain never stops changing and adjusting. You *can* learn new things and develop new skills at any age.

Wow—*1998*? Think about it. In 1981, in my master's thesis, "A Study of the Efficacy of Selected Nontraditional Healing Techniques," I primarily wrote about visualization (imagery). In 1984, I wrote my doctoral dissertation, "Imagery as a Viable Adjunct Tool in the Rehabilitation Process of the Brain-Injured Patient."

I recall talking to psychologists, psychiatrists, and social workers while doing research and writing both my thesis and dissertation. I was continually being asked, "Are you are serious? You are going to write about imagery? This is supposed to be an academic study and intellectual project. You will be lucky if your committee even accepts a draft on this."

None of the people I talked to knew my medical history. None of them were the tiniest bit aware that I was one of the most seriously brain-injured soldiers to be returned from Vietnam ... that I had once been like an animal and clawed and growled at my mother and my wife, who stayed near me at the hospital for those first thirty days.

None of these "intelligent" people knew that an imagery technique developed by a high school dropout was the reason I was able to interact with them in such a way that they had no idea I am a brain-injured person.

Patt Lind-Kyle is well aware that the development of techniques to help people create realities—ones that hardly any scientists and intellectuals could even imagine thirty years ago—was like opening up a new frontier. There is no doubt in my mind that it will be no less than a blessing to *millions* of people. Imagery is not a panacea. I still have physical limitations that I will probably have until the day I die. Believe it or not, this is okay.

Why is it okay? Have I learned to like having the physical limitations that prevent me from doing things the same way that most people can do them, like run? Of course not, but as one process is developed, I learn new things. I have different limitations and different abilities than many people have, and forty-five years ago, this was not my reality. I did not know what I did not know, and I did not know anything.

How many people can truthfully and intellectually tell you that they were once aggressive animals who now have PhDs and are married to wonderful people? I can, and I thank God for all his blessings. What's more is that every claim I make is documented. Yes, I can do this, and I believe that someday this will not be unusual.

## REWIRING

My parents did their best to help me learn to use imagery as a tool that would help "rewire my brain," help me redevelop brain patterns, which would in turn instruct my muscular functioning. And it was as if I were a newborn baby all over again; they had to start from the proverbial scratch. It seemed as though the brain patterns that once directed specific muscular responses no longer existed. Like the young athlete my father had to teach how to bat or throw the basketball into the hoop correctly, he had to help me develop new basic patterns that would hopefully make it possible for me to develop more complex neural patterns for more complex muscular functions.

It is important to understand that my parents had to motivate me constantly because I so often wanted to stop trying and give up. As some people say, call it a day. Mental activity can be as or more exhausting than physical activity. Sometimes I wanted to rest and take a long break. In my mind, I was helpless and useless. My ward mates at Madigan who were amputees were learning to walk with their prostheses, and I was having a difficult time learning to crawl. *Why should I keep trying*, I asked myself, *when I was just going to fail?*

I had one physical limitation due to my brain injury that I have largely been able to conceal. Most people did not notice, but I considered it my most frustrating limitation. At one time, I could not direct my hands to do what I wanted them to do. Consequently, during my nearly eighteen months at Madigan General Hospital, I was never allowed to eat in the visitors' cafeteria.

I could not mentally command my hands to hold the spoon (I would have killed myself with a fork), pick up food with it, and direct it into my mouth. For a long time, the orderlies or my ward mates fed me, caring for me like a baby brother. After about a year, I was allowed to eat with my hands, and of course I made a mess. No one at Madigan ever put me down or made fun of me in any way.

We were ward 13, the amputee ward, and the best I can remember is that I was only praised for what I was able to attempt, and there was always an orderly or ward mate who would hold my glass as I drank my milk. (Although a bit later, there was one person who gave me a scolding that I will never forget.)

## THE WARNING

I think I had been in the old VA Hospital in Portland, Oregon, for two or three days. Like all the patients in the rehabilitation ward, my supper was brought to my bed. After almost eighteen months of eating in my bed at Madigan, this was certainly not anything new. However, my father told me that when Madigan transferred me, they neglected to inform the VA that I had not relearned to eat with utensils very well.

I had been casually eating with my hands for a few minutes, and no one said anything to me. I was one of the first wounded Vietnam vets at the Portland VA hospital and quite young, as compared to 90 percent of the other patients. Additionally, I was the "new guy," but I still felt quite comfortable.

My ward mates at Madigan had told me several times how people in "the world" seemed to hate Vietnam veterans. They told me that civilians possibly would not bother me, because I was an officer, but just in case, I should keep my head down. I must confess that I was worried in a general anxious way, but I did not know what I should actually be worried about.

At Madigan, almost since day one of regaining consciousness, I could expect my ward mates to wheel me into the dayroom to watch television. I learned to speak from watching and listening to *Star Trek, My Friend Flicka, The Nelson Family,* and many movies.

## THE RIOT ACT

When my ward mates turned on the news programs, the war protests seemed to be shown *every single day*. Naturally, there were news stories of Vietnam veterans being harassed and spit on. I had been home on convalescent leave several times and had never been treated harshly, but just the same, I was always a bit leery that someone might want to hurt me.

As far as I was concerned, the VA Hospital was not part of "the world." Everyone I met who worked there was considerate and kind to me. There was not a single person who did not recognize that there were some things I needed help doing and who did not make every effort to help me in any way possible.

I suppose I could have tried to use my fork and spoon for this supper I referred to, but I was exhausted and simply did not have the energy to try using the utensils. Big mistake!

While I was eating with my hands and making a mess, dropping food on my bed, I noticed a woman standing at the end of my bed. She did not look at all happy. I did not know why. I was just trying to feed myself, and the angry-looking woman was the least of my concerns.

I assumed she was simply visiting a patient in the hospital. I also assumed that her anger at me might have nothing to do with me. Many people leave hospitals less optimistic, confused, and sadder than when they first arrived.

Then it happened. She said that watching me eat made her sick, and that I was the most disgusting person she had ever seen in her life. And yes, she had to say it: "And you must be one of those Vietnam veterans." She may have said more, but that is all I've been able to remember.

Regardless of what I remember or do not remember her saying, I could feel her anger and disgust. At that time in my life, I was probably (not possibly!) one of the most self- centered people anywhere, and I could not feel her pain. All I could do was feel my pain. Her body language was clear; she'd pretty much said that she did not like me. I could feel her saying I was a bad person.

What could I do? Walking away certainly was not an option. Because I did not have the ability to cry tears, I made weird grimaces and noises of some sort. In truth, I had no way to overcome the tension I was experiencing. In my childlike mind, my buddies in ward 13 at Madigan were right: the world would destroy us Vietnam vets if they had the chance, and I did not know what to do.

A grandfatherly ward mate came over to my bed and attempted to comfort me as I tried to catch my breath. A few minutes later, my parents came in the ward. When they noticed my crying, they rushed to my bed, and my father frantically asked me, "What's the matter?" I was so emotional that all I could say was, "I can't … I can't …," and with food-covered hands, I pointed to my supper covering my bed. My mother, who had seen me try to cry on several occasions, knew my grimaces were not due to physical pain, and not knowing what to do, she began looking for something (anything) that would give her an idea of what had happened.

I don't remember how long it took after seeing food all over and hearing my words before my parents seemed to come to the same conclusion at about the same time. They did not know about the visitor who had spoken to me so harshly, instead assuming that my lack of coordination when feeding myself was a big part of the problem.

Then both my parents, with tears in their eyes, held me tightly and told me they loved me and would always be there for me. I was like a child again and needed to feel them hold me more than I can describe. It felt so good. I never regained the memory of my youth, but I knew these adults loved me and would never allow anything or anybody to hurt me.

I do not remember how many times over the years my father has said this to me since then, but what he told me is something that has become a basic part of my counseling practice with physically limited individuals and their families across the United States and around the world: "Jim, I want to tell you something. It is a promise I never want you to forget. Jim, always remember this, I promise you that you will be able to do anything in the world—*anything*—if you are willing to do whatever it takes to accomplish your goal."

My father had never lied to me, and I had no reason not to believe him. When my mother told me never to forget what my father had promised me, I was more convinced than ever.

## FACING REALITY

I have faced more times than I am able to remember when I have not been able to accomplish something that I had convinced myself I really wanted to do. It would puzzle me. I felt I was really trying, but repeatedly and despite all my efforts, I failed. My failures were not a matter of not trying hard enough or a miscommunication or a misperception of what I wanted to do. Indeed, I have had times when the consequences of my efforts did not even come close to what I had intended.

Had the person I trusted more than anyone else on earth lied to me? When I asked my father if he had lied to me, he smiled. "Well," he said, "when I said you would be able to do anything you wanted to do …" After what seemed like an excessively long pause, he continued: "If that was all I said, you certainly might think that." He paused again, and this time, I was not sure if he was going to answer me or not. "But what else did I say?" he almost whispered. "What do you think I also said? Do you remember anything else?"

Of course I could remember. Hadn't he told me that if I really wanted to, he'd promised me that I would be able to do anything? If he had, and I doubt it, I felt I would have remembered it. "I have no idea …," I said.

"Jim, what I told you was, 'You can do anything, *anything* in the world, that you want to do—*if you are willing to do whatever you have to do to accomplish your goal.*" My father went on, asking me if I had stopped attempting some effort I had initiated and simply given up for no reason.

I could not remember any goals I had set out to accomplish but had not completed. My father continued: "Believe me, due to your disabilities, there are probably many things you simply cannot do. For goodness' sake, there are many, *many* things I cannot do. This is life. I cannot do many of the things you cannot do, only for different reasons.

"When we find that there are some goals that are physically too difficult for us to accomplish, we can either keep pounding our heads against a wall trying to accomplish something we are not able to accomplish or we can decide that the goal takes more time and effort than we are willing to expend. Maybe I am being overly simplistic, but I think this is life too.

"Have you ever been so confused and frustrated when you couldn't seem to do something that seemed so easy when you first thought of it?" my father asked me. "But when you attempt it in physical reality, accomplishing it seems so impossible that you get confused about what steps come after each other and get so frustrated that you almost want to spit?"

"Whatever," I replied, not knowing what point he was trying to make.

"Okay, have you ever tried something over and over and were afraid that you would never be able to accomplish whatever it was you were trying to do so you just stopped trying?" Sure I had, lots of times.

"What did you do?" my father asked me. "You stopped trying, and there is nothing wrong with that. In fact, it might be a smart thing to do. On the other hand, when you have a goal that is so important to you that you are willing to do whatever it takes to accomplish this goal, you will almost assuredly accomplish it.

"I cannot tell you what goals will be so important to you; you will do whatever you need to do to accomplish them. No one else can. Only you will know this, and as I once promised you, 'You will be able to do anything in the world if you are willing to do whatever you need to do to accomplish the goal.' Nothing in the world will be able to stop you, because you won't allow anything to stop you."

Over the years, the people I have dedicated my life to helping create their own realities have helped me realize that my father was so very right. The individuals and families I have worked with who were not afraid to change the methods with which they were attempting to accomplish their goals were the people who accomplished said goals and gave their lives meaning.

## IT MADE PERFECT SENSE

On New Year's Eve 1952, my father told me he'd quit smoking and drinking and vowed to my mother that he would devote the rest of his life to trying to be the best husband and father he possibly could. He had not had the appropriate role models in his attempt to be the husband he really wanted to be, and at the same time, he was not sure what he had to do to be a good husband and father. He had been the best soldier he could possibly be during World War II and the Korean War, and it scared him to think he might blow this effort.

After being in the army during two wars, he was pretty sure he was learning how to be an expert infantry soldier. He could do this. My father also felt sure he could teach his sons to be top-notch athletes, maybe even champions.

My brothers tell me that our father could teach even the most uncoordinated people how to be outstanding athletes. Even before psychologists and psychiatrists were talking and writing about strategic sports performance, my father had already concluded that if a person practices an effort in his mind, that person has at least an equal chance of being a success in many things as a person who only practices in a physical reality. He was just as convinced that an athlete who practiced both in physical reality and in his mind could be "dangerously" unbeatable.

To my father, practicing an effort in one's mind before practicing the effort on a baseball field, a football field, or on a basketball court made a lot of sense. He had never read a book or taken a class or workshop about "visualization," or "imagery," as this tool is often called, which I have been blessed to do.

I still chuckle when I think of how my father attempted to explain why imagery works. To my father, this made perfect sense. This is the way he explained it to me: "The brain does not know the difference between the physical reality and an image created in the brain, and it is not going to react to either differently than the other."

I think I read the same thing in some outstanding books. The words were different, and the sentence structures were somewhat more professional and academic. Still, I don't think the descriptions of imagery between the books I read and what my father told me were much different.

I will soon explain this rehabilitation tool with the more scientifically accepted terminology that academia uses to communicate with one another. To be honest, I often use this communication style to help me understand, part by part, how the tool of visual imagery operates. This seems to be how my brain operates.

Skipping the explanation of steps before I move on does not work for me. In college, I graduated from Portland State University (PSU) with a 3.53 grade point average. I never took a test I did not think I would fail. I feared that if I did not know everything, I would fail the test. I passed every test because I had already answered every question correctly in my mind before I ever walked into class. Did I overdo it? I probably did.

On the other hand, when I attempt to communicate to others *how* to use imagery as a tool that will enable individuals to improve their motor skills and learning abilities, I do not use this intellectual jargon. Many people feel these words can be impossible for them to interpret. Regardless of what style of communication is used to explain visual imagery to different groups, attempts to explain the *how* and the *what* a person can do ultimately make a difference in the way he learns (and performs) is certainly not difficult.

## HALLUCINOGENIC MOTIVATION

In December 1970, I came across a class called "Hallucinogenic Motivation" in the schedule of classes at PSU. My first thought was that it was probably some far-out class originally taught in California, which might be interesting and possibly even a lot of fun.

I am open to new ideas, and the idea of learning a new psychological theory turned me on. As I read more of the class description, I realized that it was to teach students how to use imagery to "improve skills." I figured it was probably a how-to class, which I admit I usually do not like. Still, if it discussed imagery, about which I have never found more than a paragraph in any book I had read to date, I wanted to see how different or similar what I would learn in this class would be from what my father had taught me. The class rejected the relationships to the misguided academic support or flirting with heavy drug use that seemed popular at the time in schools of higher learning, especially in California.

The reality was that it was a well-presented class that attempted to explain the efficacy of using the tool of visual imagery to do whatever a student feels is appropriate for his personal situation. My quest was to see if the imagery training could help me deal with my grand mal epileptic seizures, which were often more than I could control with medication alone.

The class was far less theoretical than I had expected, and in some ways, the primary difference between it and what my father taught me was the scientific terminology in the class, which my father certainly had never heard. I even asked my father if he knew what a neuron is, and he thought it might have something to do with gasoline. "Was I even close?" he asked. "My goodness' sakes, I have no idea what, where, or who a neuron is."

What my father, James Penny Meade Sr., *did know* was how to work with a brain-injured person such as myself and help teach the person to improve his ability to do things that he could not do at all or could not do as well previously . Without academic words, I explained to him that what he knew and guided people, including myself, to learn was how to improve motor skills beyond what most medical professionals ever thought possible. My father taught me the *how*, and the Hallucinogenic Motivation class attempted to help me learn the *why*—why using visual imagery as a tool actually works—the way mental health professionals talk to each other no less.

What my father emphasized was that if a person wants to be as good as the person can possibly be at anything, he has to "practice." This is not debatable. If he cannot practice in physical reality, the person can practice in his mind. It is possible, and it works!

During my years of rehabilitation from the injuries I suffered in Vietnam, the efficacy of using imagery in this effort has been proven many, many times. Have I always been as successful as I had hoped or expected to be? No.

As I improved in some things, it was natural for me to raise the bar for what I concluded and hoped was possible. Often I was wrong.

What I have been able to accomplish has certainly far surpassed all the expectations of my doctors in 1967!

## MIND WORK

In the December 1970 issue of *Reader's Digest* was an article titled "The Long Return of Warrant Officer Meade," written by traveling editor Joseph P. Blank. Mr. Blank wrote about how my father had built a thirty-foot wood platform with parallel railing approximately hip high. It was located in the backyard, and I used it during my convalescent leaves from Madigan General Hospital. Mr. Blank quoted my parents: "Using the railings for support, Jim tried to walk, he fell, got up and kept falling until exhausted, could no longer pull himself up. Undaunted, he crawled up and down the platform, trying to coordinate the movements of his legs and arms. He performed these exercises for weeks until he could crawl as well as a one-year-old infant."

What my parents failed to share with Mr. Blank was that I would not only practice crawling up and down the parallel bars physically; I would also spend at least an equal amount of time practicing crawling up and down the bars *in my mind*. My father or mother would be guiding me by telling me what body parts to use and what movements to attempt. They would also guide my imagery efforts. They would close their eyes and tell me such things as this: "You can see your left arm stretch forward. Place your left hand on the ground, keeping you from falling down on your face, while you bring your left knee forward."

They would direct me to see and feel every movement I attempted in my cognitive reality. As my father had told me years earlier, my brain did not know the difference between physical reality and the images I was creating in my mind. I was creating new neural pathways in my brain through practicing my efforts in my mind over and over again.

I firmly believe that the human body instinctually and constantly attempts to return itself to maximal survival state. Consequently, I might have eventually learned to crawl without consciously employing the tool of imagery to assist me. This could be. Still, I feel convinced that using the tool of imagery therapy, which is what I call it, reduced the amount of time it took me to be rehabilitated. This is another important part of using the tool of imagery therapy, which my father taught me: it's ridiculous to ask others (or oneself) to practice any new skills without also asking how they felt while practicing the new skills in their minds.

When he thought about how he felt when he mentally practiced, it became clear to him that he could limit himself with his images of physical reality. In other words, while there seemed to be exceptions, it was usually difficult to create an image that was different from the physical reality in which many functionally limited people feel trapped.

Using myself as an example of what my father was saying, I could say, "I can't do it; it hurts too much, even my image of attempting the effort." My father would not respond that it was all in my head but would instead tell me, "I bet it does." How do you think it might feel if you did this [or that]?" He always had a goal in mind and would guide me at a pace that seemed appropriate for me, helping me to function well enough that I could overcome my fears of hurting myself and failing, because I was too afraid to try, even in a different reality.

He would guide me in this manner repeatedly, until I was no longer so afraid that I could not do what I needed to do in order to be successful. I felt that everything I was attempting was new to me, and I do not think I was ever not at least somewhat afraid. My father created such a trust between us that I knew I would be successful eventually. And I knew that he would not have me do anything that would cause me to hurt myself. Most importantly, I knew that if I attempted the efforts in the way he instructed me, I would be a winner!

What I have chosen to call imagery therapy is not new, and it certainly is not an idea that my parents or I thought of. My father taught me how to practice doing in my mind what I could not do in physical reality. Since he also utilized this new skill and method of learning to help children become better athletes, I imagine he might have learned this from his athletic coach when he was a boy.

When I was at PSU in Portland, Oregon, a professor in the department told me I was too involved in visual imagery and said that if I wanted to become a psychologist someday, I should forget about visual imagery and study an area of psychology that was more than a fad and actually helped people. As I recall, I am certain that he told me I was wasting my time trying to learn something that was going nowhere.

He was a professor, and I certainly had been conditioned to feel that college professors were about the smartest people around. I wondered if he was right, whether I might be on a path headed nowhere. I questioned if it might be smart to back away from studying psychology and go into some other field.

I took a job as a field representative for Hunt-Wesson Foods. I really enjoyed this job. One reason was that I had the opportunity to visit with families and individuals with brain injuries as I traveled the length of the Willamette Valley and cities on the Oregon coast. At least two to four times a year, I met someone I felt comfortable enough to consider helping with imagery therapy.

Regardless of all the negative things I was told or read about using imagery as a healing tool for both physical and emotional maladies, I was convinced of the benefits of imagery therapy. When the doctors at Madigan had tried everything they could think of and I was still dying, my parents knew there must be something the doctors had not tried that would save my life. They did not know what that might be, but my father wondered if using my brain to heal my brain might be something the doctors had never considered.

My father was not educated enough to think beyond the basics, and he certainly did not possess the academic vocabulary to thoroughly explain what he was thinking. Still, he had an idea, and he taught me what he knew.

Most importantly, my parent taught me in a way that made it possible for me to understand what I had to *do* in order to learn what I needed to *know*. The more I learned, *the more I learned!* That may sound simplistic, but that is exactly what happens when repetitive experience forms new neural pathways that connect with other neurons to create new neural pathways. This is what healthy humans do from day one of life. This is how they learn, and one does not have to memorize all the scientific data in the world to create this reality.

From what I am told, when my helicopter crashed into the trees and the rotor blade struck me in the head, forcibly knocking my head back against the metal protective plate, I had what is called a "coup-contrecoup" brain injury, in which the neural patterns of my brain were completely changed from how they had been originally. I forgot everything I had learned before the crash because the billions of patterns of neural pathways that were my memories no longer existed. Jim Meade Jr. died.

From the second I became conscious ten weeks later, I was creating new neural pathways as I had new experiences. I was blessed that I had a ward full of men who stayed in my face from morning until night. My father did not realize how important it was that my ward mates constantly asked me questions and talked to me, even before I was conscious enough to respond to them. But my parents knew that I needed to experience and reexperience an effort in my mind before I could learn to repeat it physically.

Please do not think that I have some special intelligence that able- bodied people do not have. As you may recall, the neural patterns (memories) that existed before my crash no longer exist, and what I did not know, I did not know existed or how to create. I did not know that there were things I needed or wanted to know.

Some people may think I am a bit stupid because I cannot do some things that others think are everyday activities that almost everyone else can do. Then I come along, and I not only have no idea how they are doing the activity, but I have no idea what they are doing or why they are doing it. As an example, my brothers Tim and Squeak are knowledgeable about home repairs and remodeling. I have never had the opportunity to do any hands-on efforts of this type, and I simply don't know what I don't know ... especially because I never knew it in the first place.

I feel that I am a rather typical brain-injured person except that I have seen some demonstrations of courage and will that left me feeling more than a little lacking. At the same time, I have met many able-bodied individuals who would fit into the brain injury groups I have attended—no questions. I certainly am not saying that those people are of any less worth than anyone else. What I am saying is that all of us are more alike than most people seem to be willing to admit. I might be a slower learner, but I am learning.

# Chapter 3

## Reborn

**H**ave you ever awakened after a sound night's sleep or a nap and something just did not seem right? Perhaps you were not sure where you were, and as hard as you tried, you could not figure what you were doing in that strange place. You felt that something weird was happening to you, and you felt more than a little bit scared.

I imagine I regained consciousness much as it must be when a child is born. I did not know anything. I was in a hospital bed and had no idea I was lying down, because what I was experiencing, lying down, was all I had ever experienced. I remember it, which seems strange even to me.

The first thing I can remember about human contact were the huge human eyes over my face. I was not afraid. Still, as the eyes moved, I accepted this as reality, and I could not separate anything else I saw into parts.

One of the reasons was that I had no idea what I looked like, and I had nothing to compare anything I saw with anything else. As I saw objects moving around, I could slowly differentiate one object from another. I was in a body cast and could not see over the side of my bed (or know that there was such a thing as a side to look over), and my ward mates would seem to fly from place to place and land on my bed, and every time they did, I would laugh like a child.

It was a couple of months before I realized that some people had legs, although I was extremely puzzled as to why some people did and some did not. Something that confused me even more: after my casts were taken off and I discovered that I did have legs, I wondered what good they were since they didn't work. I didn't understand why there were three groups of people: people with legs, people without legs, and people who had legs that did not work.

After several months at Madigan, I had learned more and more about my environment, and I realized that I was kept in a building with other men who had been hurt in a war. Without a memory that I had been a helicopter pilot or had been in Vietnam, I felt somewhat like an intruder, but the hospital was the only world I really knew.

My parents, brothers, and sister came to see me almost every weekend, and my wife and her parents visited me as well. These beautiful people cared for me and talked to me all the time. There was always a ward mate by my side, every second of every day. I was never alone.

I did not understand it at the time, but my brain injury was the primary reason I was not learning to walk. Unlike the rehabilitation and vocational training that my parents developed for me, in which imagery instructions allowed me to prepare for new physical efforts, the physical therapy training I had in the 1960s and 1970s was the repetition of the physical activities alone. They did not know that new neural pathways had to be created to guide my learning.

Karen Stevens (now Nelson) had to teach me how to condition or teach myself how to gain control of my legs and arms so that I could send messages to my limbs that would initiate responses.

It broke my heart that my ward mates were learning to walk with their prostheses so quickly while I was having such trouble learning to coordinate what I wanted my limbs to do. One day while my friends were playing tennis, I asked them if I could stand up without my crutches and return the tennis ball that was thrown to me. When a friend threw the ball to me, I drew back the tennis racket and immediately became uncoordinated. I jumped all over the place trying to prevent myself from falling down. My friends screamed for help, but it was no use. I crashed like a broken box.

I felt like an idiot and was worried that I might never learn to walk. Still determined to learn to walk, I went behind the gym and pounded my head against the wall. I was going to learn but simply did not know when that would be.

Even when they retired me from the army and transferred me to the old VA hospital in Portland, Oregon, I was not able to walk without support. My father was now in Vietnam and wrote me at least every week, and my mother took it upon herself to help me as much as she possibly could.

My brothers were amazed that she seemed to give me instructions that sounded exactly like my father's had. Her timing was perfect. When I learned to go up and down sidewalks, my mother would tell me to be sure to stop, lift my crutches up above the sidewalk, balance them, and then slowly lift one leg at a time. After I got one leg up and balanced myself, I would put my support forward and follow with my other leg. She would train me how to see myself following her every instruction, which my parents concluded was essential. It seemed obvious to them that their five children learned everything in stages.

When I took my first steps at ten months old, I did not start with a jaunt around the block. The reality was that I had to learn how to get up and balance myself well enough to compensate for other factors that would prevent success. She figured that I had learned to walk once, and if I was like a child all over again, okay, we would go through it all over again.

Both my parents realized that continuous mental and physical repetition of what I needed to relearn was essential. They had me form pictures in my brain of what I need to do, much like the present theories.

My parents were able to help me to visualize a moving picture in my brain that I imagined as a complete and complex reality. Karen worked as my physical therapist at Madigan General Hospital according to standards that were even more ancient than what my parents assumed was reality. Karen was a great person and outstanding physical therapist considering what was accepted as appropriate at the time. Working with brain-injured patients, medical professionals in 1967 might as well have been practicing in 1867.

My parents knew that the simple repetition of activities surely was an effort that was going in the right direction. They also knew that I might die of old age before I made any real progress. In 2012, as far as I am concerned, we are admitting the possibility that there are new ideas that could open up fantastic doors. On the other hand, we also seem to be clinging to old ideas that are almost useless.

By accident, my parents realized that if nothing got any better, they were not going to bark up the same theories that were not producing any positive results. At the University of Oregon, I was continually on the dean's list and was chosen the president of Phi Eta Sigma, the national freshman scholastic honor society. They could tell people about any of my fantastic academic achievements, but the truth was that people who met me would only see a person who could not talk very well, could not read or write, could not feed himself without making a mess, was fairly spastic, and who, even when he could be understood, hardly said anything that made any sense.

After all my time in the army and VA hospitals, my parents felt I had been cheated in some fundamental ways, because both hospitals seemed to be waiting for me to die. My father told me many years later that there was no other way to look at it. However, they weren't knowingly cheated me.

I prefer to believe that the medical professionals in these facilities were not sitting back and waiting for me to die. They simply did not know what they could do to save my life. My parents did not either, but they were not willing to do nothing. Over the years, I have met many parents, siblings, and mates who were just like my parents and were not willing to do nothing. This is important to know.

## COORDINATION

No matter how smart medical doctors or neuropsychologists are, they do not know everything. They miss some things that might be important, and they can make mistakes. Using myself as an example, as mentioned, I have a PhD in psychology, and I know I was taught well.

But there could be something I need to know that only you know—not something even a PhD or MD knows. I cannot think of a professional who would not be excited if you were willing to share whatever you could.

This may sound strange, but I had to put how my body works back together almost piece by piece. My parents told the doctors that if I was going to die, to let me die with my legs. This, however, is not the piece by piece I am referring to.

The hospital doctors apparently were doing what they could to keep me looking like a human being but did not have the foggiest idea how to make all my pieces work or, more importantly, how to make them work together. They had no idea that I needed to learn everything that makes me a human being individually, and without learning how to make these parts function together, they were not going to teach me much at all.

From what I gather, learning a new activity that involves a series of motions involves a higher level of the brain. The higher activities of planning, remembering, and learning have to coordinate in order to perform the motion. I have read this and have spent my life working with TBI victims and their families, and I still have trouble grasping this realistic theory.

My mother left high school in tenth grade but continued her education (to become a nurse) after marrying my father. My father quit high school in the tenth grade but then finished high school and took two years of college during his military career. Obviously, they were not geniuses, but they were willing to take an idea they truly believed and attempt to help someone they loved as best they could. As the devoted parents they were, they were determined to discover what they needed to do to help heal me.

What might have aided them more than anything else was the fact that they did *not* have years and years of advanced education. What they accepted as matter of fact did not have to be explained. My father knew the results of planned imaging because he had seen that two and two equaled four; he did not require some professional to tell him why it existed. My parents did not need to know why repeated planned imaging worked, but they saw it change lives, and that was good enough for them.

Most of the time, we nonmedical people have no idea why a certain medication works. If it does, that is good enough for us. If the doctor does not know how to correct the problem, sharing ideas that he has or that are being researched helps us understand possible solutions. If presented with respect, this can help create miracles that no one could have performed without God.

I still have poor fine motor dexterity in my fingers. I am writing this book by pecking at the letters on the keyboard. It takes a fair amount of time and effort for me to write legibly; I need to print slowly. In other words, as hard as I try, some things I have never been able to master since I was injured.

What I presume is that my brain was damaged in some areas that I have not been able to completely compensate for. I can walk a mile, but I cannot run ten feet without ending up diving forward. What is the solution for this? Simple: don't run! What I need to say is that I have learned how to do things that many people have chosen to call miracles. I have also seen patients learn to do things that even their own doctors, therapists, or psychologists thought they never would be able to do.

It may not seem like an important question, but does improving physical ability increase one's cognitive abilities or vice versa? I simply do not know. Like my parents, all I know is that with the appropriate training, many people cannot help but create a miracle.

## STEVEN GRACE

While living in San Diego, I worked with injured individuals and their families during the day, seven days a week, and in the evening, I attended the University of San Diego School of Law. I had already earned a PhD in psychology but wanted to see if continuously challenging my mind would increase my cognitive ability. Then my wife's cancer worsened, and I could not adequately continue my studies after three semesters to remember more than the minimum I needed to continue in law school.

Going to law school was a fantastic experience, and I enjoyed it a great deal, but I would never become a lawyer. (Had to add that, respectfully, of course.) After giving a talk at Sharp Hospital, I had the honor of talking to a man whose nephew had had a motorcycle accident a year earlier. He asked if I would be willing to visit him in a nursing home in Escondido, California. He added that the costs of my services were not a problem, and I told him that charging him anything was the last thing we needed to talk about.

Steven Grace was the same name as a friend we had in Munich American High School in Munich, Germany, and I was thrilled to discover that this was not my high school friend. The Steve Grace I met in the nursing home had been severely brain injured when he drove through a stop sign and right into a truck. He was going so fast that he drove directly under the rear of the truck, and the rear wheels ran over his head. As I recall, he was unconscious for one week.

When Steve regained consciousness, it was obvious that he was confused and did not know where he was. He recognized his parents, who had been by his bedside for the entire time, and he hugged his mother.

Steve thought that somebody had died and that he, Steve, was in the hospital to visit that person. His mother recalled that this did not make any sense to him, and he began crying. She also recalled that Steve attempted to say many things but could not verbalize clearly and made little sense.

When I met Steve two weeks after he had regained consciousness, his speech was better, but he continued to make comments which seemed to make sense to him, but at times were completely unrecognizable.

After forty-five years, this still happens to me, albeit rarely, and I could feel his pain when he confessed that he could read in other people's expressions when his speech confused them, and it made him feel like an idiot. For some people, this causes their determination to multiply, and for others, it can reduce self-esteem to an all-time low. Depending on the client, I prefer to attempt to laugh at some things an able-bodied person might want to think twice about before bringing up, and that worked well for me in this situation. I was introduced as Dr. Meade, and when I laughed and said, "I sometimes do the same thing, and it embarrasses me a great deal too," I could hear him exhale and definitely could see tears coming to his smiling eyes. "Sometimes I fake the rest of the conversation." His father told me that that was the first time he laughed since his accident.

Assuming that everything I have read, heard, or experienced can be interpreted as accurate, I am convinced that the individuals I have been blessed to work with are taking rehabilitation routes that are working more assuredly and more rapidly than almost anyone had expected. As an example, I would like to write more about Steven Grace. His speech problem seems to have mostly been a product of the confusion and nervousness, which is not uncommon for a person who has not been conscious very long. When he laughed as he thought about what I had said, this was a voluntary response that seemed to reveal an ability to contemplate his surroundings.

Contemplating an experience and voluntarily responding might be considered a higher brain level activity, and I was impressed by what this could indicate for the future. I expected an impressive recovery.

A condition that I was concerned with, however, was that control of his legs was not returning. I would accompany him to his physical therapy sessions and watch him as he would "wish" his legs to do certain movements that simply would not occur. This troubled me, and as much as I prayed that I would be able to help him learn to walk again, I honestly wondered if his problem was not way past me.

I recalled that I had faced a similar situation, but the obstacle I had to overcome was that I kept forgetting what I had to do to complete a movement, like raising my feet above a curb and remembering what to do next. For me, each curb was a completely new situation.

Steve's situation was different from the problem I had to learn to overcome. His conscious memory did not seem to be the problem. He would even verbalize his wishes so I would recognize what he was trying to accomplish.

I did not come up with a possible solution that was realistic even to me. His physical therapist and I had talked about my medical history every day, and he wondered if half the session was pure mental exercise, was there a possibility that the rehabilitation might be successful, at least to some acceptable degree? I was not charging anything for my services, and the family had informed the director that I would be working with their son. We decided that I would work with Steven every day for a half hour, guiding his metal imagery efforts immediately before his physical therapy session. I trained his parents to do this every afternoon and evening.

I was convinced that this team of Steve Grace, his parents, the physical therapist, and I would help Steve advance much faster than expecting the physical therapist to create a miracle all by herself.

Why were Steve's symptoms different from mine? One reason is that every brain is different. My TBI was general and involved my entire brain, while Steve's injury was more specific, where the injury seems to have destroyed the neural pathways of a specific function in a specific location. Finding what areas in my brain had literally been redesigned was simple: everywhere. A specific area in Steve's brain was responsible for whatever was preventing Steve's brain from coordinating the brain's higher-level activities that are necessary in order for him to be able to walk.

Steve had not broken his leg, but even when he learned to walk again, he walked with a limp that nothing seemed to overcome. This might seem strange, but since he had no apparent reason for the limp, it seems fairly certain that his brain was sending messages that were instructing his left leg to limp. He uses a cane to walk more "naturally."

To say the least, I am proud of all the individuals I have worked with. They have healed themselves. I have guided them with the help of other medical professionals and therapists. Steve has never stopped making an effort to help him better himself, and there is even greater guarantee of success.

# Chapter 4

## THE PROCESS OF PARTS

In 1977, I entered the California School of Professional Psychology to earn a PhD in clinical psychology. The VA had called me and asked me if I wanted to attend CSPP in Fresno, California. I did not yet have a master's degree, but the VA seemed to be convinced that I could do the work that would be required after earning a BS in psychology with a high grade point average despite my having a severe brain injury.

I usually joke with people and tell them that when I was asked, I told the VA that I would think about it, but my exaggerated grin gives away that I was so excited about this that I could hardly stand being around myself. Regardless of my excitement, however, something caused me to doubt myself and my ability to earn a PhD.

As far as I was concerned, a PhD is the top of the ladder, and as Dr. Meade, I wondered if I would be expected to know just about everything about psychology. As I already mentioned, when I graduated from Portland State University, I told my father that we had to get out of there fast because when they found out I did not know anything, PSU would take my diploma back. Being invited to attend CSPP in California was an honor that made me feel ten feet tall, but without a master's degree, I could not imagine how diminutive my chances of being successful had to be.

Due to having repetitive grand mal seizures, I was on a leave of absence from Hunt-Wesson Foods after three years of fantastic and fulfilling employment as a field representative. The thought of returning to the academic world was very enticing, but I wondered how much of my excitement was due to pure ego.

I feared that in discussions with the other students, I would make it obvious that I am a complete idiot. I questioned my ability to do everything up to and including boiling water, until one day a friend I had gone to college with said that being invited to attend a school to earn a PhD had to be the greatest academic honor he had ever heard of, and that I would be a complete idiot to turn this down. Did I have any idea how much I could potentially learn? I called my brother Squeak in San Diego and asked him what he thought I should do, and he said I would be an idiot if I did not accept this offer.

I wrote to my father, who was stationed in Korea, and he begged me not to be an idiot and turn this opportunity down. My mother told me that if I turned this down, I would feel like an idiot for the rest of my life.

What was I supposed to do? I could go to the California School of Professional Psychology, where I feared being thought of as an idiot. Or I could refuse this opportunity and be called an idiot for the rest of my life. The choice was not obvious. Ten years earlier, my brain had been beaten to a pulp and I had been considered a vegetable. Something did not seem right, and I did not understand. One thing was sure: I needed help figuring out what to do, and I prayed to God to guide me. The answer I got was that I didn't have to be afraid, that simple, which was the answer I needed to hear. I was going to CSPP.

## CSPP

The California School of Professional Psychology Fresno campus was fantastic. Students went to classes in the evenings and worked at externships during the day. Some of the students seemed to be somewhat arrogant, but the professors were fantastic. Unlike some of the graduate schools, the professors were able to associate personal experiences with the classes they were teaching, and the class discussions were often amazing.

In some of the classroom discussions, I did feel like an idiot, but in most, I merely became aware that I had so much to learn. I loved every second of my classes and looked forward to reading as much as I could in order to contribute to the discussions. In truth, I never thought my attending school could be such a complete experience.

Still, from almost the day I moved to Fresno, I felt sick. I tried to hide it, but on many days, I felt so nauseated that I expected to pass out. I will go a step further and reveal that I got to the point where I thought I might be dying. I lost sixty pounds in a little over a year. A psychologist friend wondered if the reason was that the temperature in Fresno was so much like it had been in Tay Ninh, Vietnam.

My doctor at the VA could not determine why I had lost so much weight but suggested I might want to take a break from CSPP for a while. This was in 1979. I hated the idea of cutting my education short, but losing sixty pounds for no apparent reason worried me, and I was allowed to take a medical leave of absence from CSPP in December 1979.

After a year, I had gained back about thirty pounds and no longer had any episodes with nausea. Returning to CSPP was something I could certainly do, but I thought that getting a master's degree from Fresno State University would be more logical and more beneficial. Consequently, I was accepted into the Rehabilitation Counseling program at Fresno State University and got a ride down to Fresno from Oakhurst (eight miles from Yosemite National Park) three evenings a week for my classes. I could not go to my internships during most of the days and did not get credit for them, but after a year, I transferred to the MA in counseling program, which I graduated from in December 1981. I finally felt qualified to enter a PhD program.

One of the attractive things about the evening course at Fresno State was that I could volunteer my mornings and/or afternoons to help brain-injured individuals and their families. I had not volunteered to help anyone since working with an automobile accident victim in 1978 and felt I was neglecting an obligation I had to serve God through serving brain-injured people in need.

## DAD'S LETTER

For the first few years after I was medically evacuated back to the United States from Vietnam, I was completely involved with my own rehabilitation, and helping other TBI victims certainly was not realistic during those years.

My parents were with me as much as possible, but in December 1967, seven months after my crash, my father was sent to Vietnam. Squeak and David were in college, and my mother did not know how to drive. In November 1967, our son was born, which slowed Kathy down a great deal. In other words, my ward mates had to be like my parents and siblings.

My father knew that this would cause my therapy time from my family to go down from as many hours as they could give me every week to one hour a day, five days a week. This really bothered him, but he also felt that his job was to be in Vietnam, where, as an infantry sergeant major, he could use his combat knowledge to save lives. (It was his third war.)

I had forgotten how to read, but my father still sent me letters, writing on the envelope that he wanted somebody to read them to me. A ward mate was always anxiously available to read the letters to me. My father's letters were usually no more than half a page long, but just knowing they were from my father made me feel as if he were there with me rather than ten thousand miles away.

In one of his letters, he wanted to tell me something that he felt had to be the foundation of anything he had ever said to me. He knew that if I chose not to use it as the basis of whatever else he'd told me, it would all mean practically nothing. My father promised himself and me that he would support every dream I had, and he and my mother would help me in any way they possibly could. If there were times I became scared or sure I could not be successful (and they did occur more times than I like to admit), my father reminded me that the last thing I wanted to be was a quitter. Being disabled has caused me to have to postpone some efforts while learning how to overcome some of my limitations and re-create more workable plans. But to me, giving up was never an option.

I recall my ward mate crying when he read me one of my letters. He was a double amputee and told me months later that he wished his father had written this letter to him.

What my father wrote me was very simple, and I have not forgotten it after all these years. In fact, my father's advice became central to my own work with patients throughout the years. This was what he wrote:

> *James, I wIsh I could be with you, but I have to fight a war and help keep soldiers alive. What I need to tell you, I hope will guide you for life, because with it you will accomplish things that other people can only dream of and certainly cannot imagine you accomplishing. When you can write me back, tell me what you think.*
>
> *What I want you never to forget is this:, "I can do anything, anything in the world. There is nothing I cannot accomplish if I am willing to do what it takes to accomplish my goal."*

My father had never lied to me and had even told me that I was his best friend. In my heart, I knew that this was a promise my father would not make if it were not completely true.

For sure, in trying to make my goals realities, I had changed my mind about many efforts, probably more times that I can count. On the other hand, I have never quit or simply stopped attempting to make my dreams come true. My father did not tell me until years later (face-to-face) that I *can* change the way I accomplish a goal so it is more doable for me and thus repeatable.

## RECOVERY IS ALWAYS IN PARTS

After over four decades, I am still a victim of a severe brain injury. Only one thing has changed: I am a severe brain injury victim who has been able to learn. And yes, there is more than one way to accomplish just about everything.

There have been many people who, for one reason or another, wanted to know what my so-called secret was. What had I done to change myself from an animal-like TBI victim to the person I am today? I once would say that I must have a secret but simply have not been able to figure out what it is. If you are going the typical and accepted rehabilitation route of the professional community that is often shared and that stresses the "only way" to rehabilitate a TBI victim, then, yes, I may have a secret you may not have considered.

The first part of the so-called secret is that while the TBI victim is in the typical confusion state that lasts for whatever amount of time after regaining consciousness, he does not have the ability to process anything that is more profound or complex than a basic comment or command. For some victims, like me, it does not simply come back; it is a relearning process that has to be created.

Remember my mentioning how after a couple of years of going to parties for disabled individuals, my brother informed me that it is not appropriate to kiss the hostess good- bye on the cheek? My behavior was "socially unacceptable," but this was something I had constantly seen on TV (with the Nelson Family, on *Leave It to Beaver*, and so on), and I was never told that this is not always acceptable, especially among complete strangers. Again, I did not know what I did not know. This had been wiped clean from my memory and had to be relearned. If I did not relearn the social rules, it would be as if they never existed.

The relearning is like a process that progresses from the most basic and then, possibly, to the more complicated, depending on the degree of the brain injury. This progression takes as long as it takes.

The second part of this that should not be a secret is that no one can truly rehabilitate anyone else. My family and many other people have attempted to guide me as best they could. They would often tell me what I needed to accomplish and expect me to remember the instructions I had been given. In days past, this was considered rehabilitation, as if role memorization were not a choice that needed to be prompted.

The TBI victim has to picture the process of an effort and be able to consciously coordinate the individual parts of the effort. The victim necessarily coordinates the parts. The helper guides.

The third part is that no one can be rehabilitated alone. Don't get me wrong. No one can rehabilitate you, but professional therapists are possibly more important than just about anyone else at this point, although loved ones can be even more important, because they foster an emotional component that can support a will (more than a desire) that will accomplish miracles.

It is important to keep a communication channel open with the professional who will help you and avoid unwittingly saying or expecting things that could be negative, if not destructive. A confused TBI victim often lacks the awareness to discriminate the possible meaning of words, misunderstood facial expressions, what may seem like conflicting tones of voice, and even comments between other people that they have possibly only partially heard.

For TBI victims, expecting someone else to rehabilitate you and at the same time expecting to be rehabilitated without *personal* effort is 100 percent of the time a guarantee of failure. That simple!

Remember what my parents told me? If you are willing to do what it takes to accomplish your goals, there is nothing you cannot do! The opposite is just as true. If you are *not* willing to do what it takes to accomplish your goals, it makes sense that you are not going to learn how to do anything.

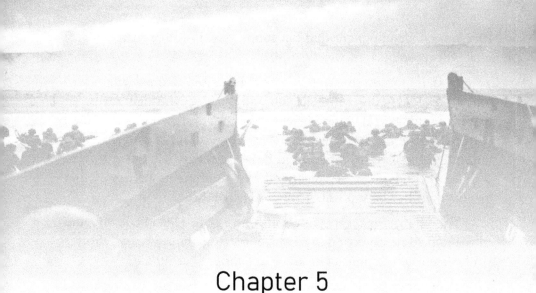

# Chapter 5

REENTERING THE WORLD: THE BEGINNING OF MY LIFE

**I**think I can imagine what it must be like for a baby coming into the world. You might recall that I woke up to a world that was completely new to me. I wonder if I was more amazed by what I saw than what I did not see, for my brain injury prevented me from being excited by anything.

The eyes I first saw looking down at me seemed huge, and I had not yet learned to differentiate the parts of the face. If I could not be excited, I still think I was curious. In my reality, these were the first things I had ever seen in my world.

Because I was in a complete body cast, my world was restricted to whatever I could see above myself, which was probably an emotional blessing, for seeing the entire room and the people in it might have been emotional overload. As it turned out, as far as I could determine, the amount of completely new stimuli I experienced must have been perfect, because I don't remember being anxious or stressed in response to anything I experienced.

Everything I was experiencing was completely new to me, and I feel that God created the condition where all I could do was experience the world around me in parts. I could not see myself, had no awareness of what I could be, and consequently experienced myself as a part of everything my eyes experienced.

Not realizing that I had a head and face and eyes, to me the world around me merely existed as a whole, and my eyes floated me around it. Thinking about it now and recalling what it seemed like, I can only recall complete peace at the time. I was all my thoughts and nothing else.

This was the beginning of the only life I know; the rest of this life of mine has been a story of adaptation and acceptance. My first world was probably a ten-by-twenty-two-by-twenty-foot space above me, which must have been stimulating enough to prepare me to experience the world that surrounded me.

I was totally amazed by the reality around me. There is no other way I can express it. As I recall, I felt nothing else, although the truth may be that I did not know how to express anything else. I was in excruciating pain, but my body had not redeveloped the ability to cry, and my mother remembers the first time I laughed, about a half year after my return to the United States. Like any animal in a box, my world was restricted to the corners I could see. Unlike even an animal, however, I could not touch the corners and had to assume they were real. I could not even touch myself. Yes, a little bizarre, maybe even completely weird.

After they removed my body cast and replaced it with casts on both legs, my physical world greatly expanded. My father and mother had fun joking about how I did not know what a window was. I could see out the windows from both sides of my bed, but I had no idea there was an outside of the ward. Seeing people walking outside the ward flabbergasted me. My world ended and began at the door of the ward, and I wondered what was beyond it. It seemed that my family would visit me and walk away to nonexistence. I must confess that that was so funny!

My world was more than quadrupled in a matter of less than an hour, and more information was made available to me by the minute. My mind had more stimuli to add to my brain, and the combination of new stimuli to the old made my existence more exciting. I never forgot my experience with the room's brightness. It puzzled me. What was this aura that enveloped me and kept my excitement from turning to fear as my curiosity increased?

I began to realize that I probably looked like the friendly creatures that were constantly on my bed and talking to me. I accepted this, and wondered which of my ward mates I looked like.

It has always amazed me that I have remembered so much of this part of my life. A psychologist friend once told me years later that having all my previous memories erased may have allowed my empty mind to rapidly form neural pathways from new memories and new information. He told me this was conjecture to explain something he could not even imagine, but I must admit that that is the only thing I can imagine also.

## NOT ONE ANSWER

Cutting away my leg casts opened up another world to me, something strangely confusing. Being rolled out the door and through what seemed like endless hallways to the room where the doctor cut off the casts seemed to be a ride that would never end. When he cut the casts off, all I experienced was the buzzing noise and a tickling sensation that was completely new to me.

Dr. Marx was curious about why I was excited about my right leg and indifferent about my left leg. I forget what questions he asked me, but I found out later that he realized that because I could not feel below my left knee, I was completely unaware it existed. I never talked about my left leg being numb, because I never thought about it.

I was pushed in a wheelchair back to ward 13. Talk about a trip! I kept thinking I was going to slip out of the wheelchair, I saw that there were more people than I had previously thought possible in the entire ward. I am told that I was grinning so broadly that all people could see were eyes and teeth. Physically I could not cry, but the excitement I was overcome with was more than I thought possible. My ward mates would push me to the TV room and take turns taking care of me, talking to me about everything they could possibly think of. They would turn on the television and use programs to teach me how to talk again. The TV became my door to the world.

A year or so after all my casts were removed, I was wheeled into the psychologist's office, which was in another wing. I did not know what to expect. One reason was that I no longer had any idea what a psychologist was.

He was nice to me and smiled a lot, but I couldn't figure out what he expected of me. No idea. What is the name of the state you are from? (What is a state?) No idea. What city do you live in? (What is a city?) No idea. What is the name of the governor of your state? (What is this?) No idea. What is your father's name? (Father?) No idea.

There were ten questions, and after all this time, I still remember those questions. I could not answer any of them. Even though I could not answer one, I can remember at least five of the questions.

It seems that everything I was experiencing was forming new neural pathways that created my new memories, and everything I added to my memory must have fit together perfectly. Additionally, my massive brain injury seemed to have created a situation where for at least several months, I could not create or react to stress. The world merely happened.

Over the coming months, I would attempt to learn to do what I saw the people around me do. This became very important to me. Without a past, I felt like the man who fell to Earth, and I was willing to do whatever I needed to do to be like the people I saw and met. To me, it was never a question of whether or not I came from the world. I did not.

Obviously, unlike my ward mates, no one was coming to take me home for good. I accepted this even though I did not know why nobody took me home. Maybe I would find out. Until that day came, this was home.

It made perfect sense to me. I was in a place where they kept men who had been in a war. I had never been to this war (it was completely out of my mind), and somebody had left me here for a reason I must have forgotten. Had I done something? What was my mission?

I had taken information that seemed to explain my questions about myself and anything else, and to give myself any meaning and purpose for being, I *created* a world (or worlds) that enabled me to validate the reality of any perception I had of anything.

The men in my ward, Kathy, and my family took wonderful care of me, and at the same time, I traveled along self-created paths that I needed to take in order to survive.

## CREATING WORLDS

My family must love me, for they have always been there for me. No one recovers from a brain injury quickly, and most people never recover completely. Putting this in a way that is more factual, I do not think that anyone who has experienced a brain injury is completely symptom-free. Most people who have suffered a severe brain injury take years to recover and *never* recover completely. I cannot stress this reality enough.

After I was discharged from Madigan General Hospital and the old Portland VA Hospital, the Veterans Administration sent me to Mt. Hood Community College. I had barely relearned to read or write (and my IQ score was so low that I could not stay in the army), but I had spent almost two years at the University of Oregon before joining the army. Apparently, because I had been on the dean's list every semester and had been the president of the U of O chapter of Phi Eta Sigma, Mt. Hood had to accept me. On paper, I looked good scholastically.

My parents had told me repeatedly what a beautiful brain I *used to have,* and I was determined to do what I needed to do to graduate.

It took me six quarters to improve my reading, writing, and math skills and to complete the two quarters of transferrable classes I had to take in order to graduate. But I graduated. Yes, I graduated with a B average no less.

I practically studied all day, seven days a week, but I had to prove to my family and mostly myself that, although I am not the same person that I supposedly used to be, Jim died in Vietnam, and James is here! Were there times I doubted myself? I would not go that far, because I knew I was willing to do what I needed to do to graduate. At the same time, however, there were times, maybe many times, when I wondered if the shell I had created around myself was really worth it. I drove away Kathy, after all she had done for me, and I had not given myself permission to make any friends. I felt like a loser, and I attempted suicide in 1970.

That same year, my brother David, a Special Forces lieutenant, was killed in Vietnam—three years and one week after my crash. (May is not my mother's favorite month.)

I have never been able to remember growing up with my brothers, but David was a beautiful person and wrote to me on a picture: "Jim, all our lives we have been pretty much alike, and I want to be an officer, just like you." He made any memory I created of my past that I might have had special beyond words, and I miss him very much.

Remember how I mentioned that some effects of brain injury never go away? Even though I attended David's funeral at Willamette National Cemetery, for about eleven years, I believed that my brother was not actually dead and instead was badly wounded and in a VA hospital in the Midwest. I believed this with all my heart.

Major Jack Saint, my cousin who had been an instructor pilot when I was a student pilot and had flown two tours in Vietnam, escorted David's body home and told me that David had lost a leg in Vietnam.

I took this information about his leg, and this became part of a new truth: he was ashamed to come home. For eleven years, I waited for David to come home. There was no doubt about it in my reality. He was my friend and he was coming home. Yep, David was coming home. I needed to believe this. Vietnam had taken everything from me, and I could not live with the fact that David, my little brother, had been taken from me too.

Marie-Louise (my wife at the time) and I lived in the city of Oakhurst, in the beautiful California foothills. It was 1981. We were sleeping when I suddenly jumped out of bed and started crying and screaming, telling my wife, "I was sleeping and had a *vision*. David, yes David, came to me and asked me if I would like to visit him and his friends in heaven. So I went up to heaven and joined them as they played cards in a circle. We were talking and laughing and having a great time. I don't know how long it was, but it was great. David looked like what my brother looked like, and visiting him was a wonderful experience. I was leaning over a hospital gurney, and a man came to me and asked if the one I was on was mine. I was caught by surprise and said, 'No, I'm just visiting.' Sweetheart, as soon as I said this, I woke up and ended up back here in bed, and I know this is the last time I will ever see my little brother."

I cried harder because I truly believed that this was the last time I would ever see him, at least until I joined him in heaven. I could not stop crying off and on for another two days.

I accepted the fact that I might have been dreaming, although I had no idea why I would dream something that would mean I would never see David again.

Want to know something? I am being completely truthful when I say that there is no reason whatsoever that I would dream something that would nearly kill me. I don't care if I am asleep or not. In my heart, I believe I will see David again. I will also see Squeak and our Dad again.

Another point is that I cannot dream. Brain injury or not, if I created this reality, so be it—it was my reality!

## PORTLAND STATE UNIVERSITY AND SPEECH DEVELOPMENT

A handful or so of us met every day for coffee at one of the rooms in the student union at Portland State University in downtown Portland, Oregon. We usually discussed classes we were taking, with a bit of small talk about anything that came to mind. Pat was an honor student, as was another girl and one of the fellows. Although we talked every day, none of us knew each other beyond our daily coffee.

After my first semester at PSU, a professor of one of my classes advised me to take speech development so that when I spoke in class, people might be able to understand me. He was blunt when he told me that knowing the material means absolutely nothing if I cannot communicate my knowledge to anyone else.

Of course, he was right. My speech instructor at Mt. Hood Community College had told me that I deserved an A plus for my guts and for talking to the class, but he was giving me a C because it was "so darn hard" to understand me sometimes. He was being kind to me.

The *Reader's Digest* article about me had not come out yet, but he had learned my story from my records.

My friends at PSU never discussed my speech problems, but I knew I had issues communicating. My own father had told me that my speech could drive people nuts, and my brother Squeak once told me, "You might want to do something about your speech problem." I could not hear my speech deficiency, but as much as I did not want to admit it, I knew that if I did not get help, I might be sorry.

Taking the speech development class was definitely one of the smartest things I have ever done. I learned that one of my problems was that I did not breathe correctly. (I still cannot, but it must be due to my emergency tracheotomy in Vietnam). I also spoke much more rapidly than was necessary, which prevented me from enunciating clearly.

After two semesters of speech development, my self-image was 100 percent better. When I get tired, my ability to speak clearly goes down several notches, and speaking too rapidly is as unclear as ever, but when I do what I was taught to help me speak clearly, people have even complimented me.

I possibly would have graduated with or without this help, but I can talk to people without sounding like an imbecile, and this feels good. All because I was willing to do what I needed to do to accomplish my goal. Many of the people who complimented me probably heard me talk a couple of years earlier. They did not want to say anything earlier that might have offended or hurt me. This is what I felt they were really saying when they praised me: "James, I remember when your ability to speak really sucked; I felt really uncomfortable, and this is my way of getting it off my chest and telling you. Am I being obvious?"

Yes, you are but guess what. I presumed that my speech did not impress people before the speech development program, and I thank you for noticing the difference. I have tried so hard to speak like a normal human being, and what you are telling me is that my efforts are paying off. Thank you so very much.

I do not notice it when I am tired and sometimes do not speak clearly, even now. When people start telling me they are so proud of me for how hard I attempt to speak clearly (repeatedly and unexpectedly), I usually get the message.

## My Psychological Defenses

While counseling people for over thirty-five years both in groups and in the Lieutenant David E. Meade Memorial Centers, I noticed that one big reason I had trouble completing some goals is that I myself didn't really want to accomplish the goal. Saying "I can't" is a no-no that drives me to find out why I cannot do it and how I can compensate for whatever limitations exist.

I simply told myself, "I don't want to anymore" and attempted not to think about it. One problem is that I know I was trying to fool myself. Deciding to join the speech development class, which was only me, was not this way. I knew I needed it; I simply did not want to spend my life speaking as unclearly as I did.

But I am nowhere near perfect, and I am no different from any of my patients that I have worked with for over thirty-five years. I had found ways to talk myself out of ideas that I had convinced my wife or family were pretty good.

My brother Squeak is the only person who told me he recognized my pattern. To him, it was obvious. I was willing to give my all to complete most efforts, but even I have limits. And limitations are what many people seem to have difficulty understanding, even about themselves.

It is as if some of us are so much into denial that we do not want to admit that there are some things we simply do not want to make the effort to accomplish. Most of the time, if I begin a project, I feel a need to complete it. This is to show myself and my family that I can do it—and that I will.

I determined that I *would* learn to dress myself. I wanted to be like my ward mates. All we had to do was put on our gray pajamas, robes, and shoes. It was easy for my ward mates but impossible for me. They could zip through it, while I could not get my pants over my feet and up my legs. I can remember not being able to figure out why I could not pull my pants up to my waist while in a sitting position.

Shirts were worse. I will not even begin to get into what this was like. When I look back now, a smile comes across my face, because I know what it is like to be convinced that there is no way in the entire world I will *ever* get *both* of my arms in the *same* shirt. I was having fun with the ward nurse one day, and I doubt she will ever forget how I assured her that I would not go to vocational rehab unless I could go naked, because only crazy people wore clothes.

It was obvious to me that I had to learn to dress myself especially since, in this life, I had never heard of a nudist colony. I also needed to learn to feed myself, to read and write, to use my wheelchair, and to talk. Watching my ward mates, I decided that learning how to comb my hair was important. I finally learned to turn on the TV and received a sitting ovation. I was so proud that they were proud of me.

Trying to learn to play tennis without my crutches (or with my crutches) was not a need but 100 percent ego. I was going to show a couple of my ward mates who were playing tennis with their artificial legs that I could stand in one place so that when they hit the ball to me, I could hit it back.

Watching them, I was sure I could do this, even though I had no idea what I would do if the ball did not come right to me. I did not have the cognitive ability to know that even if I wanted the ball to come directly to me, there was a chance it might not.

I do not recall how far from me the tennis ball came, but when I stretched my arms for it, I fell right on my face. I knew the ball was coming in my direction and recall felling as if I were in another world as I tried to locate it in space. It was a bizarre experience.

Hitting the ground face-first knocked me silly but not unconscious, and my ward mates rushed to me, scared half to death. They were screaming for help, and I started fake laughing, pretending nothing was the matter.

This was the first time I was aware that I had ever failed at any effort so completely, and it was the first time I became aware that I might fail at some efforts. This had to happen eventually, and this may have been as good a time as any. On the other hand, I wonder if I had to learn of my vulnerability by attempting an effort that was completely unnecessary and ridiculous.

For the rest of my life, starting right then, I have been a bit reluctant to attempt new things and felt I had to be aware always of the consequences of failure. Strangely enough, I thought about this even when I was unable to think clearly for a matter of years.

My ward mates had told me so much about helicopter pilots and Vietnam that I developed an extreme pride that I had been part of something they thought so much of. For me, however, my brain injury destroyed my memory of being a pilot or having flown helicopters in Vietnam. In other words, in my mentality, I had never been to Vietnam. In my reality, I had not forgotten my Vietnam experiences. They never happened.

I accept the reality of my past. My parents have boxes of pictures of David, Squeak, and me as boys, living in Trieste, Italy, and going to high school in Munich, Germany. I don't remember a second of them and probably never will. I am sixty-five, and my world seems to have begun forty-five years ago in Madigan General Hospital.

## GRADUATE SCHOOL AND HUNT-WESSON FOODS

After earning a bachelor of science degree in psychology at Portland State University, I attended Western Theological Seminary in Portland and then became a sales representative for Hunt-Wesson Foods. Seminary was not as great an experience as I had dreamed, mostly because going to seminary directly after five years of college year-round was something I had a hard time adjusting to.

Hunt-Wesson Foods was a fantastic company to work for, and I truly loved every second I worked for them. After a couple of months of training, I was given a silver Chrysler for a company car and transferred to Salem, Oregon, where my area of responsibility became the entire Willamette Valley, south of Portland, from I-5 on the east to the Pacific Coast to the west. I had a home built in Salem for my wife, and our first daughter, Dava-Lee, was the first child born in Salem on New Year's Day 1975.

I could not imagine ever living a more fantastic life. I visited wholesale companies monthly and spent the rest of the month moving Hunt-Wesson products from the wholesalers to retail grocery stores. I loved meeting the people I sold to and was ready to spend the rest of my life with Hunt-Wesson Foods.

I made a point of not mentioning my Vietnam experience, and the people I worked with in stores thought I had an accent, although they never asked me where I came from. One grocery store manager asked me if I ever had been in Europe, and I told him I had lived in Italy for four years and Munich, Germany, for four years. That's all I said, and he never asked anything else.

When I became ill, it was completely unexpected. I had already had epileptic fits two or three times over the years, but for some reason, I started having seizures one right after another, or "status epilepticus." This went off and on for several months, and again I was told I was going to die. Hunt-Wesson was great and put me on a medical leave of absence, continuing to pay until my social security benefits began.

## INTERNATIONAL COLLEGE

As a student in the University Without Walls program of International College, credits earned from accredited schools of higher education are credited toward graduating. I took classes at the California School of Professional Psychology for four trimesters, took classes at California State University Fresno for two years (year-round), and took classes from Sacramento and San Francisco campuses for two years.

My PhD in psychology is fully accredited by the Department of Education, the State of California. Graduates of the PhD program at International College are eligible to earn the Marriage, Family, and Child license and the Psychology License. I am also certified as a hypnotherapist. At Fresno State, I passed all the academic requirements for a master of rehabilitation degree and then transferred to the master of arts program in counseling, where I earned my master of arts.

Marie-Louise earned her PhD at CSPP in 1970, and we moved to Oakhurst, California, about eight miles from the South Gate at Yosemite National Park. When she earned her PhD, I had a year left to complete my master's degree at Fresno State.

# Mt. Hood Community College

The Board of Education of Mt. Hood Community College, with the recommendation of the faculty and by virtue of the authority vested in them, hereby confer on

## James P. Meade, Jr.

the degree of

## Associate of Science

with all the honors, rights, and privileges thereunto.

Given at Gresham, Oregon, in the month of June, one thousand nine hundred and seventy.

Chairman of the Board

President

# Portland State University

Portland                  Oregon

On recommendation of the University Faculty, and by the authority of the State of Oregon, Portland State University hereby confers upon

## James Penny Meade, Jr.

the degree of

## Bachelor of Science

with all the rights and privileges appertaining thereto.

Given on the fifteenth day of March, nineteen hundred and seventy-three.

Chancellor

President of the Board

President of the University

*Diplomas of Mt. Hood Community College and Portland State University.*

SIERRA MEADOWS CONVALESCENT HOSPITAL

## SIERRA MEADOWS CONVALESCENT HOSPITAL

Sierra Meadows Convalescent Hospital is in Awahni, just a mile or so from Oakhurst. I do not remember if it was June or July 1980 when I called John Ralf, the director, to ask him if there was a patient there with whom I could be allowed to work. I gave him a copy of the *Reader's Digest* article about me, copies of my transcripts, a copy of an award I received from President Carter, and my resume. I also told him that I would visit the patient every day and not expect a dime for my services.

He asked me why I wanted to do this (especially for free), and I told John that this is what I do. "I am the most blessed person I have ever known of or know, and I have obligated myself to helping people in need." As I recall, John immediately knew the person he wanted me to work with. He told me that he would have to contact the patient's mother and ask her for permission for me to work for her son before giving me his name.

What he could tell me was that the patient had been in a serious motorcycle accident two years earlier and could not talk or feed himself, nor could he walk or do anything to take care of himself. He did not tell me that the patient was tied down by all four of his limbs, could be violent, and had been sent back by two major rehabilitation hospitals that said they could not help him.

I honestly believe that John was afraid of driving me away if he had told me the complete truth, which would not have been unexpected. What I would have told him is that outside of being told a rehabilitation hospital could not help me, what John told me about the patient at Sierra Meadows could have been how I was once described. I also would have told him I have never worked with a violent client but would claw and growl at my wife and mother only thirteen years earlier. Nobody abandoned me, and I was not about to abandon anyone else.

**California State University, Fresno**

The Trustees of The California State University and Colleges
on recommendation of the Faculty
have conferred upon

**James Penny Meade Jr.**

The Degree of

**Master of Arts**

Counseling

with all rights, privileges and honors thereunto appertaining.

Given at Fresno, California, this twenty-fourth day of December,
nineteen hundred eighty-one.

*Earning my MA degree in counseling at California State University of Fresno, and membership to the California State Psychological Association.*

Upon recommendation of the Faculty of

# International College
## Los Angeles, California
and under authorization granted by the
California State Department of Education
the degree of

*Doctor of Philosophy in Psychology
in the University Without Walls program*
is hereby conferred upon

# James Penny Meade Jr.

together with all the rights, privileges and honors
appertaining thereto.

Given this **24th** day of **June**   nineteen hundred and **eighty-four**

Francine Bennett Ph.D
Tutor

President, International College

*I earned my PhD in Psychology, program at the University
Without Walls, International College, June 24, 1984.*

John asked me to come back in two days. He was sure that that would be plenty of time to get the permission I needed, but if not, he would call me and let me know what might be a better time.

As it turned out, John had to fax my records to the patient's mother, and this caused the visit to be in three days instead of two, but I knew how protective my parents had been of me and had expected to have to wait much longer.

On the day of our meeting, I arrived an hour early at a restaurant that was in the middle of Oakhurst, about a half mile away. John had called me the previous evening to tell me that he and two nurses had read the information I had left him, and they were anxious to meet me. John added that he had a strange feeling that I might be the answer to many prayers. I responded that I was not a miracle worker by any stretch of the imagination, but I knew this is what I was meant to *try* to do.

The first thing I did when I walked in John's office was ask the patient's name. He was a human being, and I wanted to call him by his given name as soon as I could. He said that his name was Ed Ruby and then went on to tell me the same information he had told me on Monday. One of the nurses told me that she'd prayed I could do something for Ed because the way he was right then was so sad—he couldn't do anything.

When we got to Ed's door, I noticed that he was bound by all fours just as I finally had been told he would be. But from the very beginning, he looked at me. I was a stranger, and he was curious. This gave me the idea that Ed had the mental ability to pause and contemplate his environment. He also growled at the nurses as if he wanted them to do something.

When I sat in a chair near Ed, something happened that set the stage for the next couple of years. Even with tied-down hands, he was able to grab one of my hands and try to bite me. He was helpless and was telling me this ticked him off.

I had not worked with biters before, and I looked Ed right in the face and told him, "You bite me and you will be the sorriest person in the world." If his brain injury had destroyed his ability to interpret what I said, it would have made no difference what I told him. If he could interpret what I said, I felt confident that he would respond to me in some way.

This is exactly what he did. He stopped growling and looked at me with a stunned look. I said to him, "Ed, you know what I just said, don't you?"

He smiled at me, and I knew everything was going to turn out just fine. There was no doubt in my mind. I felt honored that I could be a part of another effort to help a traumatic brain injury victim live the best life he possibly could. I'd suffered a severe brain injury, which means an "extended unconsciousness and amnesia after injury." Over fifty-two thousand Americans die of a TBI each year, and the Brain Injury Association has estimated that a survivor of a severe brain injury may require between at least 4.1 million to 9 million dollars of lifetime care.

Yes, I am truly blessed. I know what it is like to have friends disappear and be left alone when I needed them. Don't ever doubt that survivors gain from knowing that they are not alone. This is so very important, and it is important that people take the time.

## WHAT A DIFFERENCE

I returned to begin working with Ed the next day and was amazed that he was extremely excited when he saw me at his room's door. The nurse's aide who was taking his vital signs told me that Ed seemed like a completely different person and was very anxious for me to visit him.

The nurse had told her about me, and she told me she wished me all the luck in the world. She also did something very professional; she made a point of saying the same thing directly to Ed to let him know she would be there to help us in a second if we ever needed her.

She told me later that she had never actually spoken to Ed the person before but felt that today it might be important. What insight! It might have been two years since anyone except his family spoke to him as a real person of worth, and I wondered if he communicated his frustration and anger by being violent and yelling.

From the moment I entered his room, his eyes were fixated on me, and if he was like I had been, he needed my recognition and was prepared to respond, even if he could only make noises that only had meaning to him.

Ed probably desperately needed to hear me say anything, to ask him something and to *praise* his response. The way he reacted to what I'd told him the previous day had caused me to feel rather certain that he understood everything I said. He knew what he wanted to say but no longer had the ability to talk.

As was the case with me when I was in that situation, I felt that Ed could not "hear" that what he said to me was garbled. It would take time to train his facial muscles and his brain to work together well enough to speak clearly to anyone. Communication is like a two-way street of receiving and responding, and Ed was on his way.

Ed was a highly intelligent person, and it puzzled me that two rehabilitation hospitals had concluded that they were unable to help him. From our very first meeting, Ed seemed eager to better himself. Some of his garbling lasted minutes as (I think) he told me about himself, and even if I could not interpret his words, his changing facial expressions revealed a calmness and purposefulness that told me complete stories.

Before the end of one week, Ed had learned to pronounce and demonstrate that he could understand the meaning of several words. For a couple of hours every day, I would have him close his eyes and see himself pronounce words, even see himself making short statements. He would see this in his mind repeatedly. Then, when Ed felt he was ready, he would actually practice saying what he was conditioning his brain to remember.

I was so proud of the effort he was making to improve himself, and I thanked God for the privilege of being his guide. Although I did not recognize this at first, each day he would add at least one or two new words that he was fairly sure I had not asked him to practice the day before. When I recognized any word he attempted, I would praise Ed for how well he was learning to speak.

Unbelievably, by the end of two or three months, Ed had learned to make two- or three-word sentences that were both understandable and appropriate. Truthfully, Ed was advancing so fast that I was no less than amazed. From the very first day and every day, I repeated to Ed what my father told me: that he could do anything he wanted if he was willing to do what he needed to do to accomplish his goals. I told him that this is the reason I can do what I can do, and Ed must have been able to understand this long sentence, even if he could not repeat it.

After three weeks together, as John Rolf was walking by Ed's room, he heard Ed yell, "Hi, John!" This is more special to me because I was not there. Ed had chosen the appropriate time to say hi to John. Ed had been in complete control, and this was proof to me that he was willing to do what he needed to do to accomplish his goals.

## TIME CREATES LIMITS

Ed had done so very well the first months of my visits that I could imagine all the things I felt so sure he would be able to accomplish. It had been thirteen years since the helicopter crash, and most people could not recognize that my injuries were more than minor ones. I could only imagine what Ed would be able to accomplish in thirteen or fourteen years.

Ed had the desire, but in some situations, desire simply is not enough. Sometimes it is more important that others praise and support people, for the fantasy is enough to make life feel worthwhile.

He practiced feeding himself every day, with me guiding his mental imageries, which we worked together to create over and over again. He was learning to feed himself with a great deal of coordination, and with each new day, he got better and better. It even reached a point where his seemingly effortless motions seemed automatic, and his occasional smile while he fed himself seemed to reveal his pride at perfecting another skill.

We should have considered this possibility much sooner than we finally did, but Ed had been unable to walk for so long that his legs atrophied. And as much as he tried, he never was able to learn to walk. He was never able to straighten his legs to the degree he needed them to be.

In other words, while I cannot run no matter how hard I try and have reached a point that I do not really care, Ed apparently will keep trying as long as there is a dream.

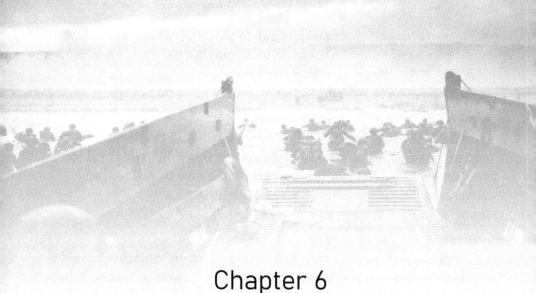

# Chapter 6

## WGSQ

From 1974 to 1977, I worked for Hunt-Wesson Food, and until 1981, I was on medical leave. From 1975 to 1981, I counseled disabled individuals and their families. From 1977 to 1981, I was also a student at California School of Professional Psychology and California State University at Fresno. From 1981 to 1984, I was a student at International College and took classes and studied at CCSP, Fresno State, Sacramento State. From 1981 to 1984, I also worked with disabled individuals and their families. In other words, no matter what else I was doing, I continued fulfilling my promise to God and my obligation to people who needed and wanted my help.

As was also my promise to God, I never charged a penny for my services. Being retired from the army and getting compensation from the Veterans Administration for being 100 percent disabled, as well as having a psychologist wife who wanted to help me and felt that she was part of what I was doing, we developed a budget that made it possible for me or both of us to be there for an average of four to six people a year.

From 1984 to 1986, I had a twenty-month internship to get a license as a marriage, family, and child counselor in the state of California, of which I loved every second. I worked for the Vietnam veterans and their families at the VA Vet center and the Fresno Vet center. I also visited Indian Vietnam veterans in the Sierra mountain foothills. The Vietnam Veterans of America invited me to meet with Vietnam veterans at the San Quentin State Prison. Even as I walked from the parking lot to the gates I would have to bypass to get inside the complex, I was so excited that I could hardly walk a straight line. I was not a bit scared, but I was afraid that they would not talk to me, a stranger or whatever they would choose to label me.

As it turned out, the prisoners there seemed to do everything they could to make my visits productive, comfortable, and pleasant, obviously something I never expected.

The warden must have given them my records and the *Reader's Digest* article about me, "The Long Return of Warrant Officer Meade," because the inmates were allowed to show me anywhere I wanted to see except inside the building that contained death row. Geronimo Pratt led me around the campus, and as we passed the building, he said, "This is death row" with no emotion whatsoever.

All I could think was, *My dear God, I can tell this to my children, grandchildren, or anybody else … and who would believe me?* I told this to Geronimo, who answered, "I would believe you."

Geronimo Pratt and Jim White showed me their cells, though I was not allowed to enter them, just look through the doors. The cafeteria was huge, and I was not allowed in the yard or near the track.

I will never forget my visits to San Quentin. I never met a prisoner or a staff member who was not nice to me, and I never saw an interaction between a prisoner and a staff member that was harsh or negative in any way.

One reason for my positive and warm feelings concerning my interactions there has to do with the banquet the Vietnam veterans had honoring me and the other Vietnam veterans with me. It was like almost any other banquet I have attended, except it was at San Quentin! There were speakers who said the same usual things, of course, honest but often a bit corny and always with terrible jokes.

They also made me an honorary member of the San Quentin Vietnam Veterans Group. I think I almost started crying (although I cannot cry tears). They also presented me with a light blue hat with the letters VVGSQ on the front of it.

Even after all these years, I still wear it from time to time, and when people ask me what the VVGSQ stands for, I tell them the Vietnam Veterans Group of San Quentin. "It is a group of fellow Vietnam veterans. They fought in the same war my father, my brother, and I fought in—and the same war that my little brother died in." I am as proud to belong to VVGSQ as any other group I am a member of.

I am also a proud member of the Scottish American Military Society, Vietnam Veterans of America, the Clan Campbell Society, the Military Officers Association of America, and the Military Order of the Purple Heart. I qualified to be a member of the latter on April 27, 1967, eleven days before the crash that ended one life and made the beginning of another possible.

## BEING UNIQUE AND NOT ALONE

I say something that most people do not want to argue but that some people have a difficult time accepting. It might be because of the statement that most people are more alike than different, which I have heard many, many times.

The statement I often make is that no two people in the world are exactly alike. In other words, everyone in the entire world is different, fundamentally different in ways that make us all unique. But we are the same in so many other ways.

My family tells me that I am a completely different from the person I was before my helicopter flew into the trees in Vietnam. They have never told me how I am supposed to be different and have cut short any discussions about my being different. This is not difficult to accept. We are the product of everything that has happened to us from second one of our existence. This is why we are all unique creatures. All of us perceive and interpret everything we experience differently, even if in a somewhat similar way.

Our existence is a constant continuation of responses and free will and on and on until the day we die. Everything we do or experience affects an interpretation and a reaction to the next.

When the rotor blade battered my brain, it wiped away the neural pathways of memory that were whoever I once was. I do not know why this had to happen to me, and I think this is what happens, to some degree, to anyone who suffers a traumatic brain injury. My brain cells were slammed with violent force to the back of my brain, and just as violently, they slammed into my skull at the front of my brain. To put it crudely, everything was knocked out of place. Everything about Jim, except the memories of others and pictures, ceased to exist.

I have no memories of "me," because they do not exist, and because the memories of the past do not exist. In my reality, it is as if they never did. I have met many people with little memories of their pasts and have never met anyone who could remember the incident that caused a traumatic brain injury.

I am the only person I know who has completely no memory of his past. To be truthful, there have been times I wanted to think a memory was original, but it always turned out that what I thought I was remembering was no different from what my family had described to me.

(I cannot see in pictures in my mind, in response to the same words they gave to me gives the chance of an original memory away.) For sure, I would give anything in the world to be like other people who have a path that can tell them all the places they came from and allow them to create futures. A part of me tells myself that it would be so fantastic.

I have written in other places about the one time I was sure that I came from another world, another reality, and fell to Earth. After discovering that there is a book with the title *The Man Who Fell to Earth*, it may be safe for us to assume that this is where I got the idea … from the title. Still, I gave in after realizing that the reality of my origin is probably the title of a book, and I still wonder what my reality is.

Like so many people experiencing post-concussion confusion, I can put this fact together with that fact to mean something that is validated with a third fact that may, in reality, have no connection to the previous facts and create a reality that I must decide is real.

Are we crazy, as some people may assume? Many people do put two and two together and are satisfied with something that is close to the number that seems most acceptable. For most people, this seems to be their reality. These people consider this creativity.

A brain injury can cause this reality to be more possible. What do I mean by this?

Remember what I wrote about my acceptance of David's death. I attended his funeral at Willamette National Cemetery and saw his casket. My parents talked about seeing his body. Even for me, this was definite proof that it was my little brother being lowered into the grave.

I have visited with patients who seemed fairly lucid yet could not recognize a family member or a friend who came to visit them; they would loudly demand that the person leave the room. Some of these patients were angry and scared, positive that the visitor was going to harm them. I have seen this break more than one heart.

The most common response is that a TBI victim is crazy. I have visited patients who, for varying periods, could not remember who I am or why I was acting so friendly. These people seemed to be doing fairly well in every other way, at least cognitively. They were polite and nice to me, and they felt that I had a good reason for being there, but for the life of them, they could not figure out what the reason could possibly be. A couple of times, the patient would laugh and tell me that he knew he should know why I was there but was "completely blank."

It might seem unlikely that these TBI symptoms are almost never completely non-recurring, even after the victim seems to be recovered or well. When I have these moments, I can sense that something is not the way I feel it should be. Still, even if I feel as if I may be in a daze, and I sense that what I am feeling somehow, in some ways it is valid and the true reality. I may question it, but if the mental experience is more than a product of my imagination, I do not want it to stop existing.

## Making a Reality

These images are created in the mind of the TBI victim for a reason. It has been my experience that they self-create to alleviate the pain or frustration that only the creation of a new mental reality can alleviate. I experience pain every day. I can usually only sleep five or six hours a night because I become aware of the shocking pain that will not let me fall back to sleep.

Some days I cannot speak clearly no matter how hard I try. I cannot write legibly, but I can print, albeit slowly. Sometimes printing is so frustrating that I would rather be doing anything else. Sometimes I get so frustrated that everything tastes like I am told cardboard tastes and tell myself (and truly believe) that I am not hungry. Even though I have been told that I need to eat on a regular schedule every day, I cannot experience hunger.

My body was so torn up in Vietnam that my being severely brain injured was as much a blessing as anything. Imagine this: I was torn up so bad that the doctors at Madigan General Hospital were contemplating amputating my legs, but my TBI was so severe that I was not aware of my injuries.

I did not know where I was or why I was there. A radio reporter interviewed the men in my ward several months after I joined them.

Even though I could only answer ten single-word messages, when I was asked where I was wounded, I mentioned both legs, both arms, my throat, chest, and gut. He knew this, but nobody was rehabilitating my head, and I had no idea that that was why I could not talk clearly or why physical and vocational rehabilitation was going so slowly.

My ward mates would joke with me that I was just a klutz. I had not reached a point where I'd figured out that being a klutz was a negative way to describe a person. It was obvious to me that my ward mates could do things that I could not even dream of, but my reality was that I would keep trying until my efforts were acceptable, which I felt had nothing to do with me. Things would get better merely because they were. I could not understand that things can be made better. This was my home, and the furthest thing from my mind was that I was getting better in order to leave. Having no idea that it was ever any different, what was there to change? And why? Enough with "why." *How?*

## THE BRAIN HEALING ITSELF

I completed my master's thesis in 1981 and my doctoral dissertation in 1984. My master's thesis was titled "A Study of the Efficacy of

Selected Nontraditional Healing Techniques," which primarily included the use of imagery to enhance or possibly cause healing to occur. My doctoral dissertation was titled "Imagery as a Viable Adjunct Tool in the Rehabilitation of the Brain-Injured Patients."

While putting together my thesis, I was repeatedly advised to change the subject I wanted to study and write about. To everyone I talked to, imagery was a fad and not something I should waste my time on. The consensus of mental health experts at that time was that they were opposed to the idea that imagery research could produce anything worthwhile. Most medical practitioners and psychologists viewed practitioners of imagery therapy techniques as harmful quacks.

When I shared that I had designed my dissertation around the idea that imagery could be a tremendous tool in helping brain injured individuals, some fellow PhD students as well as professors actually laughed at me and told me I obviously was not prepared to do serious academic research. I recall a person telling me that she would not be surprised if my committee read my dissertation draft and decided not to meet with me.

Truthfully, I must confess that I was taken aback when these comments were made, even to the point of wondering if I had not been fooling myself all these years. Was everything I had read little or nothing more than fantasy? I had been working with brain-injured individuals and their families since 1975. I never charged anybody anything, but still I wondered if maybe I was guilty of quackery.

I reviewed my notes of all the patients I had worked with. One of my standards in accepting individuals as patients in my imagery therapy program was that they had to have been rejected by a rehabilitation hospital program or a professional—an MD, MSW, or PhD. Again, Ed Ruby had been sent back to Sierra Meadow Convalescent Hospital from two rehab centers.

My goal was to help these individuals do things that they had been told they would never be able to do again. None of the people I worked with were able to recover all of their abilities, as I always hoped will happen, but I feel that all of them were able to recover some skills in ways that were important to them. An important fact that I have learned from the TBI victims I have been honored to work with is that survivors greatly benefit from knowing they are not alone, that someone recognizes their worth as human beings. I am a retired army helicopter pilot (with emphasis on "retired"), and if my wife agreed to return to work, I would volunteer to visit people.

All these things went through my mind. My parents and siblings helped me become the person I am today, but because they are family, I never asked if my learning skills that no one thought I would be able to master again was anything special.

When the people I work with learn new skills, I can get excited. I have seen them overcome their pains and fears. When I overcome mine, they no longer exist and I forget them. I remember them when I want to remember, but most of the time, I merely continue living. I am proud of myself for what I have accomplished, but if all I do is think about what I have done, I will live a boring life and be a boring person. I've never met people who have told themselves that when they grow up, they're going to live boring lives and be boring people, and I would rather that not be me either, if possible. I do not understand why I can remember my life from when I regained consciousness on so very well, like remembering the questions I was asked on the short IQ test and, at the time I was asked, not being able to answer the questions.

Take brushing my teeth, for example. I never grasped that cleaning one's teeth is important. Watching my ward mates, I simply decided that this was something I would do also. It makes me laugh when I remember how amazed I was, while on a thirty-day leave home, that my brothers brushed their teeth also, and I could not remember them being in the hospital except to visit me.

## IMAGERY THERAPY

In introducing myself, I explain how imagery therapy seemed perfectly natural to me. My father could not remember where or when he learned it. It was not anything special that only intellectuals understood. As I said, both he and my mother quit school early.

My father went to Alaska when he was eighteen years old and was a foreman by the time he was nineteen. During World War II in the army, he went from corporal to staff sergeant after two months and two weeks in combat. Rejoining the army in 1949, he proved himself as an expert at anything he attempted, and after thirteen years in the army and getting a waiver for not being in the required eighteen years, he became the third person in the army to be promoted to sergeant major E9.

As a coach for dependent baseball and basketball, his team was always a league champion. My brother Squeak was a US all-star Little League team member, and Squeak and I were members of the Babe Ruth champions of Munich, Germany, and Europe. Squeak also attended Pacific University on a baseball scholarship for his entire four years.

My parent had been teaching my brothers, sister, and me the same thing all our lives. They felt that they certainly were not as smart as the doctors who were treating me, but at the same time, when the doctors at Madigan told them that they did not know what to do to save me, my parents told me they did.

They had raised five children through childhood, and their oldest son (me) was back in what was the equivalent of childhood. They were going to raise me exactly as they did the first time. They were going to teach me everything they could about doing everything I did not know any longer.

My father was the initial coach and motivator. Then he left for Vietnam for a year and a half and was a command sergeant major of the Americal Division. As mentioned, he wrote me a letter every two weeks, and somebody read them to me. Everyone at Madigan knew me or about me. My ward mates made sure of that, and every time someone read one of his letters to me, up to a dozen men would listen. (I told this to my father, who got a big kick out of it.)

What he told me (promised me)—that I would be able to do anything in the world if I was willing to do what it takes to accomplish my goal—has remained a cornerstone of everything I attempt to do. A friend once told me that I work harder at accomplishing things than anyone he has ever known. I appreciate what he said, but I had to answer him, "Oh, there are many people who work as hard as I do or harder, and there are lots and lots who are smarter than I am and figured out how to do things quicker and better than I, but there is no one in the universe who has to work harder than I do."

I am so blessed. Some people may choose to call it being naive or a consequence of being brain injured, but during the first of many years of rehabilitation efforts, I had no idea that anybody had to make less of an effort than I did. I had no memory of anybody having to accomplish *anything* any other way than I had to. In other words, the way I did it was the way you do it. I was born into this world the way I was, and my ward mates certainly weren't the best examples that others do anything the "easy way." Sometimes when I look back over the first thirteen years or so of my life after the accident, I'm surprised that I haven't driven myself up a tree. I also know that the men I attempted to mimic at Madigan were an image of determination that I have never found anywhere else.

I have to add something important. I was injured on May 8, 1967. It took me over twenty days to be medevaced from Vietnam to Madigan General Hospital. About seven months later, my father joined the Americal Division in Texas, and a month and a half later, he was in Vietnam, the same day as the infamous My Lai massacre.

Many years later, my father told me that they flew over My Lai that day but had no idea what was going on below them. With tears in his eyes, my father attempted to motivate me, for he knew that he had to be in Vietnam helping other soldiers stay alive. Even if I was a warrant officer and a helicopter pilot when I was sent to Vietnam, I was only nineteen, and my father felt even more meaning in doing what he felt he had to do. I was a kid who had learned to fly a combat helicopter.

## MY FANTASTIC MOTHER

My mother was fifteen years old when my parents were married in 1943, shortly before my father was sent to the Philippines. On January 19, 1947, when I was born, my mother was eighteen years old. Although I do not remember what I have chosen to call my first life, I am told that our relationship, in many ways, was as if we had grown up together.

My grandfather had put her in an orphanage when she was four years old, after my grandmother died. She was there for six years, until one older sister and her husband were able to take her home with them. Five years later, she married a "tall, good-looking Indian stud" and lived with my father's parents in Banks, Oregon, until my father returned from the war with a case of malaria and a slight wound behind his left ear.

They divorced in 1971, and my father would often tell me that for twenty-eight years, my mother was the greatest wife a man could have. Part of being a great wife is being a great mother, and I cannot imagine anyone being a greater mother than my mother is.

When I returned from Vietnam, my mother, father, and my brothers (Squeak and David) were there to meet me at Madigan General Hospital. They did not know what to expect. My father once told me that they had received a call informing him that I had died in Japan and then received another message that I would be in Oakland another day because I had a high fever and was still unconscious.

While my brothers and father walked the endless halls of Madigan, they stopped to look down at a wounded soldier who was unconscious but hyperactive. He was in a body cast, and his face and skull were completely bandaged. My father told my brothers, "This soldier is torn all to heck." He had too much on his mind to wonder why such a badly wounded soldier would be in a gurney out in the hall. Of course, the soldier was waiting to be put in a room.

They continued walking and finally returned to the main offices, where a doctor met them to take them to the intensive care ward to see me. The doctor was to be with them when they saw me and to let my family know that they would do everything they could for me. I had been unconscious from the second the rotor blade hit me, and I was in no pain.

When they walked into my room and saw me, my father said he wanted to scream. The soldier they had seen in the hallway was me. My mother, who was an emergency room nurse, determined right then that if I died, it was not going to be until they had tried everything they could think of to save my life.

One of the men who drove me by ambulance from McCord Air Force Base to Madigan told my father, who was in uniform (but not knowing he was my father), that they did not think I would survive the eight-mile trip from McCord to Madigan.

*Picture of Dr. James P. Meade, Jr.'s mother, Christine (Williams) Boyed.*

Even as an emergency room nurse, my mother had never seen a person as torn up as I was. She knew that traumatic brain injury victims were most often kept comfortable while hospital staff and family waited for them to die.

She read books on brain injuries and called people around the country, attempting to gain whatever information she could. She filled notebooks with things she would teach me to do, such as teach me how to walk and talk, read and write, feed myself, and so forth. She kept meticulous notes that she wanted to give me someday.

In her notes, she told me her stages in completing the efforts, which we discussed years later. My mother would discuss what she felt she needed to accomplish, and she told me what my father had to say about practicing an effort in one's mind to ensure a successful physical reality. As I did with TBI victims later, they instructed me in every segment of an effort.

Karen Stevens would teach me in physical therapy at Madigan to move my hand forward as I attempted to crawl and then bring my leg up behind my hand. This activity would be repeated over and over, until I was exhausted and could not continue. The object was to condition my brain to repeat the same motion on almost an automatic basis.

Of course, my brain injury almost guaranteed that this would take me much longer than the average non-brain-injured person, which I am sure Karen realized. Another reason that traditional physical therapy took so long (or at least longer than mentally practicing an effort) was simply that some patients were tired halfway through a session. The longer they practiced after reaching a certain point, which varied with each patient, the less likely they were to use the practice effort constructively. A tired brain is less likely to retain a complete image of an effort, regardless of what the image is. The tired brain is naturally going to interpret an effort less directly, and a subsequent effort attempted will only be as imperfect instructions the brain transmits.

When it was time for me to relearn to feed myself, my mother first taught me to close my eyes and see the food in front of me. I needed to see where the food in front of me was in space, where it was on the table, where it was in relation to other foods. What did each food look like? I was to attempt to become fully clear where everything was in my mind and in front of me.

The first thing she wanted me to do was be completely aware of the food in front of me. She was not going to ask me do something or leave me not knowing where I needed to find something. Later, in a future session, she might ask me to pick a green bean, and I had to be able to instantaneously find that bean, know it's shape, know how to pick it up with a spoon, know how to lift the spoon up and through the air, and know how to move the spoon so I could put it in my mouth instead of hitting my cheek with it. I also had to know how to move the spoon out of my mouth and down to the table. I was to lower my hand and arm until the spoon was on the table, and then I would release it. We do this very thing naturally and are not generally conscious of each individual step of our efforts.

Everyone who has the ability learns to interact with the environment systematically while growing up. Most children have learned to walk by themselves by the time they are around a year old. My mother tells me that I was walking by myself, in my first life, before I was eleven months old. In my second life, it took me over three years. It took me over two years to learn to feed myself without making a mess.

YOU SHOULD KNOW

By now, I think it is clear that my parents were convinced of the brain's ability to train and heal itself about thirty years before academic and research professionals began stating that this could be an important possibility. In 1967, the year I was medevaced from Vietnam, this idea was considered little more than a joke.

My father knew without a doubt in his mind that mental imagery was a tool to rehearse physical efforts with the mind, and this tool can be equally as effective as hands-on practice. When the doctors said they didn't know what to do, my parents were prepared to take charge and make every effort to save my life. More than that, they were determined to make it possible for me to live a positive life.

Over the years, I have read dozens of books to help me understand how the brain functions and how people can do what is necessary to help themselves. It seems that almost all the books I've read say the same thing, only in different words. Different writers, even professionals who have authored several popular books, emphasize different brain parts as essential functions to understand.

This, of course, is often little more than not saying anything, because this complex organism is in reality a conglomeration of parts, if you will, that operate together and cannot function independently. Any brain injury makes this obvious.

After years of research, I have chosen to call the work I do and have done for over thirty years "imagery therapy." This is the simplest name I can think of. A complex description of words I cannot pronounce or remember in an intellectual game is not something I want to be part of.

My parents took what made perfect sense to them and told me what I needed to do to make my life worthwhile to me. The love and constant attention I received from them, my wife, the doctors and nurses and medics, and my ward mates saved my life. I was unconscious for ten weeks, and imagery therapy does not work by osmosis. Imagery therapy, a directed mental effort, is essential.

Whatever anyone chooses to be God, I choose to believe the unknown factor that saved me is God. I never stop giving the credit to an innumerable number of factors as contributing to saving in my life. In my heart, I believe that God directed all these forces to work together.

I am what I am primarily because of what my family and ward mates did for me. They searched for information to describe what they were doing and could not find a thing. Still, they knew what I had to do. They knew they were guiding me and motivating me, and that only I could do what had to be done.

I have worked with seventy-five patients who seemed to qualify for imagery therapy. What was essential was that instead of waiting to be treated, the patient had to reveal to me that he might be fully able and determined to heal himself and make the effort required.

When I first began working with brain-injured patients, I only had a bachelor of science degree in psychology. I knew what worked, even if I didn't know why it was working. My history attracted many patients who knew I was counseling families of brain-injured individuals. In my heart, I never doubted the efficacy of what I was doing, but I did not have a license of any kind to do what I was doing, and I never called myself anything that was not appropriate. "I am a counselor with a BS in psychology and thank you for contacting me," I would say.

I required a couple of things. The victim and her family or loving group had to work together, and there had to be somebody with the victim when I worked with her. If someone was going to help the victim, I wanted that person to witness what I did and be able to mimic me.

They all had to promise me they would work together and practice at least twice a day without me. Additionally, as mentioned, all my patients had to have been diagnosed as being unable to be rehabilitated by another professional source, and I promised them that if they were willing to do what it takes to accomplish their goals, I would help them as much as I could.

Then I would repeat my story and tell them that I would work as many hours as it seemed appropriate to both or all of us at no cost whatsoever. I told them that I did not ask to be compensated in any way—and that the only condition was that they were to agree to tell no news agency of our arrangement.

Someone told them what I do, and this is the only way I can keep myself to one patient at a time. I have never had anyone insist on paying me, and I have never given up. This was my obligation to God, and they seemed to have no problem with this.

## PATIENTS

Something I need to stress again is that no two people have brains that are exactly alike. No two people have traumatic brain injuries that are alike. Before I write another word, you probably know what my next statement will be. No two traumatic brain injury victims will respond in the same manner to the same treatment. It simply is not possible.

Patient CR6 was a twenty-eight-year-old male who suffered a disabling brain injury after falling off a roof on which he was building a brick chimney. At the time of our initial contact, his major complaints were his inability to talk clearly, which he attempted to conceal by laughing constantly and often inappropriately, and an imbalance that limited him to walking slowly and for only two or three steps before feeling he was going to dive to his left side. He could see out of both eyes, but if his left eye was covered, he could not see a thing. There was no apparent damage to either eye.

He would feel unbalanced when he tried to walk, write, feed himself, dress himself, or even talk to someone and look the listener in the face. It also seemed he was experiencing what seemed to be exaggerated bouts of anxiety, pain, and fear almost constantly and without apparent reason. What was extremely puzzling to me was that although his desire to take an active role in his rehabilitation efforts seemed sincere, he would become extremely agitated, and occasionally mildly violent, at the experience of pain or even excessive discomfort and would cease making an effort. It was interesting that after these demonstrations of frustration, he would almost invariably deny being frustrated or acting out.

After visiting him several times, I still had a difficult time concluding what would be the most productive imagery I could design. Sometimes a simple image seems to be most helpful, and I preferred this, but this is not always so. Complicating my final decision making, the victim's primary care provider had decided that speech therapy would be appropriate. I agreed with this, but he neglected physical therapy, vocational therapy, and psychological counseling, which seemed even more necessary to me.

Speech therapy almost assuredly would have helped his self-image improve, at least to some degree, but this is one's social self-image. Most speech problems are not completely discernible by the TBI victim, while what he cannot do is often painfully obvious.

The victim's inability to remain motivated to act in the face of pain or excessive discomfort, however, might have been an indication that the victim did not feel academically or experientially qualified to successfully attempt to correct the problems I mentioned. I suggested that he be referred to a psychologist to help him deal with these issues.

The doctor decided that the victim/patient could not speak well enough. He certainly had acceptable reasons for making this decision.

While I would have made a different decision, a medical team has a leader to lead, and I was blessed to be a member of the team.

The best medical team discusses as many issues as come up, and after being part of many teams, I realized that the best teams are the ones where all the members work together. My role was to help him remain motivated in the face of excessive discomfort and help him design images that would help him improve his abilities of walking, talking, writing, feeding himself, and dressing himself. To do this, I worked with him twice a day for an entire month and expected him to practice with his family or friends at least another two times a day. I made a point of stressing that working any less could possibly make our entire effort worthless.

To help improve his ability to walk, I thought he should image prancing across a tightrope for three minutes. The primary reason was that he feared he would fall and hurt himself … or even worse. Patients can sabotage their efforts by telling themselves that no matter what they do, they're going to hurt themselves. However, after repeatedly experiencing being in complete control, this is rare.

If he imaged slipping and falling while walking the tightrope, the patient was to put his being in complete control into action by willing the image of falling, catching the tightrope, and pulling himself up again and continuing the walk on the tightrope. This image was to instill in his unconscious mind that nothing serious would happen if he did lose his balance, because he had the control he needed.

Being struck by a truck and thrown over thirty feet against a brick house could leave almost anyone a little leery. A person might fear almost anything, and in this case, the victim feared not being able to speak clearly again. I had him image himself as a human dummy with no human ventriloquist talking before a huge audience where it was essential that people in the last row of seats heard his every word. After two weeks, I told him that he was to see himself talking in slow motion. After a little over three months, it was amazing how clearly he enunciated a majority of his words.

Despite my effort to help improve his physical ability to write/print more clearly and more effortlessly, the dexterity in his hands did not seem to improve, as was the case with me. My fine motor dexterity has gotten better much more slowly than I had hoped. We worked with his hand dexterity problem three to five times more often than his other body parts. We met for over a year, and even though his hand dexterity slowly improved, it probably happened naturally and had little or nothing to do with me or my help.

On the other hand, we were able to do something that he'd been told he would never be able to do again. With this, his self-image improved to such a degree that it was obvious that he might never need my help again. Where once he was afraid he would never again be able to function in these areas, he realized that if he was willing to do what he needed to do, he clearly could accomplish just about anything.

After working with this person daily for over fourteen months, I actively solicited for critiques regarding the victim's progress and prognosis for future improvements from the victim's physical and vocational therapists, psychologist, and family physician. Every therapist was willing to say that the time necessary to retrain the patient was one-third to one-half the time they felt would be necessary shortly after they first met him. His psychologist could not find any time to respond, unless I agreed to pay for the hour he needed to read his notes and the additional hour to write the report, which I did not. The family physician told me that he would not write a report but wanted me to know that he really liked working with me. I can live with that. His notes to the family complimented me as an important part of the team.

## ADVICE GIVEN

This may seem strange to many people today, but I have called my mother specifically for her opinions regarding some of the TBI victims that I have worked with, and many years ago, she made it clear that she would not offer me advice. I was a person that these people came to for help, and she was not going to interfere with my relationships with "the most important people in the world."

One thing she has always advised me to do is put myself in the shoes of all the people I've worked, with which I have been blessed to be able to do almost 100 percent of the time. Even when I felt the most different from those who had asked for my help, I recalled moments or situations I experienced that seemed, for one reason or other, similar enough to help me think of some definite possibilities.

The first thing she always asked me was what the victim's self-image seemed to be. She knew there were times when I did not think I could accomplish anything. I simply did not know how to do many things that most young people automatically learned to do, and I would be wrong to assume that the victims I was working with were different than I was.

For a while, my world was restricted to an area of no more than ten or fifteen square feet. I remember when my speech was terrible, but I did not know it was. People would say words to me, and I would utter sounds back. I would say things that, to me, were very clear. I can even recall times when I simply could not understand why people wouldn't do what I wanted them to do. As I learned much later, it was not unusual to feel that people didn't understand me. When I really needed something, I was convinced that nobody wanted to help me.

One of the reasons it took me so long to learn to walk was because I didn't have the ability to balance myself well, and I was constantly taking a dive in some direction that was beyond my control. Because of my brain injury, I did not merely fear falling on my face. I anticipated falling on my face and hoped that next time it would not hurt too much. What I experienced and still do sometimes is common for brain injury victims. Physical therapy is only the beginning of what a brain-injured person needs. Karen tried to teach me how to move my leg bones, but my battered brain fought her all the way, and in the midst of it all, I feared and waited for my next dive into the bushes. I knew exactly what the person I was working with was thinking. At least I'd experienced so much of the same thing that I had a good idea. I asked questions. Sometimes what I concluded was wrong, even way off. Then I asked more questions. I am so blessed to often be right on. I have learned to be the person I am, every bit of me, and God has helped me help people find the people they want to be. They have to do the footwork themselves, and I give suggestions. Every person has his own words that motivate him. The secret is to listen.

## DNIPROPETROVSK STATE UNIVERSITY

In 1989–90, I was the founding president of the San Diego, California, chapter of Vietnam Veterans of America. Believe me, this was an honor. The Vietnam Veterans of San Diego organization also provided me with information and support that I truly needed. Just from talking to me, these fellows knew that I did not have any idea of the basics. I wanted to form a chapter of the national Vietnam Veterans of America organization, and I am blessed that they helped me when I did not know what to do.

I was also working with a TBI victim in Santa Sedro, a section of San Diego, and had to find extra time for chapter work, which I simply did not have. This was not going to win me any friends since my working with TBI victims at no charge was something I only shared with my wife, but I was hoping another Vietnam veteran would be willing to take my place almost from the very beginning. The Vietnam veterans I met were important to me. The TBI victims needed me to help them help themselves, and there were too many wonderful people who gave of themselves to help me for me to do any less for anyone else.

As VVA chapter president, I was invited to meet a group of Russian and Ukrainian Afghanistan veterans that the State Department was taking to different cities throughout the United States. We were going on a boat ride in the San Diego Bay, around parts of Coronado. This was an honor I had never even dreamed would be possible.

It had been about twenty-three years since I had been in Vietnam, but I could empathize with everything they said about their war. Somebody had told them about me, and they treated me like a hero, which I told them was not the case. I have worked very hard to overcome my injuries, but the real hero was my little brother, who was killed three years and one week after I was injured.

The boat ride was meant to be a day of fun for these men, and we talked nonstop for the entire trip. Then one asked me if I would like to teach at Dnipropetrovsk State University in Dnepropetrovsk, Ukraine. He had graduated from the university there and knew some people in the administration. He felt that there was a better than average chance

2066741

МІНІСТЕРСТВО ОСВІТИ УКРАЇНИ

ДНІПРОПЕТРОВСЬКИЙ ДЕРЖАВНИЙ УНІВЕРСИТЕТ

Д Д У

№

м. Дніпропетровськ

James Kedde, Jr.
868 Mc Vey Ave. No 58
Lake Oswego, Oregon 97034
U S A

     The Dniepropetrovsk State University invites you
to teach English and Psychology in 1993-1994 academic year
(since August 28, 1993 till June 5, 1994) to the undergraduates
of the department of Psychology and English. You will be paid
an average salary of a professor of the University (40.275 krb.)

President
of the University                       V.F.Prisniakov

*Letter from the Vice President of Dnepropetrovsk University.*

111

that his school would invite me to teach there if I applied. He asked me if I had a business card, which I did, and he promised me that he would get back to me in a couple of weeks. I'd gone to high school in Munich, Germany, and had seen much of Europe and Asia, but being completely honest, I never expected to hear from this fellow or the university. I'd dreamed of teaching in Ukraine, but I was sure this was no more than a pipe dream.

About two months later, almost to the day, there it was: a letter from Dnipropetrovsk State University asking me to apply to be a visiting professor in the psychology/English department. I could hardly believe it. The current professor was going to China to be a visiting professor there for two years, and there would be an opening they would be happy to have me fill.

I had been a certified California community college lecturer in psychology for eleven years and had taught for the San Diego Community College District and Mesa College for five years, but being a visiting university professor anywhere blew my mind. After thinking about it for thirty seconds, I began putting together my transcripts from the University of Oregon, Mt. Hood Community College, Portland State University, Fresno State University, the California School of Professional Psychology, and International College, which is now Sierra University. I had never thought about it before, but all of a sudden, my years of studying all seemed worth it.

During my educational career, the rewards of my efforts had been my grades and being recognized as a scholar by being on the dean's list. At the University of Oregon, I had been elected president of Phi Eta Sigma, the national freshman scholastic honor society. Still, this was an honor based on what I did right then, and thinking about it was like it brought tears to my eyes. I wished my brother David could have been there to share the excitement with me, and in my heart he was. When the university wrote me back, I was a little hesitant to open the letter at first, wondering if this had all been a dream. Still, I opened it. All it said was that Dr. James Meade Jr. had been accepted as a visiting professor at Dnipropetrovsk Preprocessed State University for the 1993–94 academic year. I would be paid the same salary as any staffer professor.

I was thrilled. This was October, and I was to be there August 1993, ten months later. Not knowing what could happen in that length of time, I decided to pack my underwear that same day and my clothes the next day. As it turned out, I am sure that I packed my bags twenty to thirty times over the next ten months.

Writing about the next two years could fill this book because it was a true adventure. It has been said that teaching in that part of the world is a different world than in the United States. Not even close. It's a different universe. Every day after class, students would go to the library and spend hours sharing books to prepare for the next day.

Discussions I listened to in the psychology/English classes were extremely open. This astounded me because a Ukrainian friend told me that three years earlier, the psychology/English department, which is in a separate building, at least three or so miles from the university campus, was where they trained spies!

I recall a meeting with my students and friends when they came to my apartment and Andre was introduced to me. I thought my friends were teasing me and introducing me to another American. His English was perfect American English. I had students who spoke with excellent English accents, and Andre was a member of the graduating class. Andre became my translator when I talked to Ukrainian businessmen, and his parents became good friends. Andre's father was a retired major in the Russian army and had spent his career working on the massive Soviet railroad system. He could not speak a word of English, and I could only speak enough Russian to get by, but we got along great.

Andre's mother spoke perfect English. Notice that I did not say good English. She spoke better English than anyone I've ever met, and I spent much of my life where very good English was expected. I do not remember meeting a Ukrainian I did not like.

From October to April, it would snow every night, and from April to October, my students and I would eat ice cream and drink coffee outdoors at a restaurant about a block away from our university building. We would laugh, talk, and have a great time, and I loved every one of them. Except for my best friend, Andre, all my friends were Afghanistan veterans, widows, and my students. I would have stayed there. But I didn't.

## ECONOMIC UNION OF UKRAINE

My first year teaching at Dnipropetrovsk State University was truly fantastic. I wonder if my students were trying to impress me with good to perfect English, and I feel sure they were. I also spent a lot of time with my translator, Andre, and his wife, Eva, talking with businessmen who were in the transition from socialism to capitalism. I spent much time with men and women who had spent their entire lives manufacturing products that were sent to Moscow to be finished and then sent back.

Communism is a political system, and socialism is an economic system. The people had rejected communism, and I wanted to know what kind of an economic system they were attempting to create. My students would sometimes come with me, and I was amazed by their awareness and, equally as often, their ability to make so many thought-provoking statements.

At the end of 1994, the Economic Union of Ukraine director at Dnipropetrovsk State University asked me if I would consider being the US representative to the economic Ukraine. I mentioned that there are zillions of people in United States who know much more about business than I will ever know. The director responded, in perfect English, "Yes, probably so, but they did not care enough to come here and see what it is like in Ukraine today. You did. You are the kind of person we want, because we trust you. We trust you to care about Ukraine, because you already do."

How could I argue that? My first thought was, *Boy, have I got him skunked.* Then I realized that I do care, and I wondered how many other American people could say the same. I accepted his invitation. When I told my father that I had been invited to represent the entire United States to the Economic Union of Ukraine, my father said, "See, you can do whatever you want if you are willing to do what it takes to accomplish your goals."

I did not know I was going to be asked to represent my country, the United States of America, to the Economic Union of Ukraine. I'd gone to the Ukraine to teach psychology. I was so excited that I could hardly stand myself.

Dr. James P. Meade, Jr; International Director    May 30, 1995
Meade, Robinson, Branch International
3262 SW Lake Grove AV.
Lake Oswego, Oregon 97035 USA

Dear Dr. James Meade,

The Dnepropetrovsk Regional Board of the Economic Union of
Ukraine would like to offer you the position of official
representative of the Economic Union of Ukraine ORB for the
United States. The position will require you to represent the
EUU to manufacturers who would consider doing business in
Ukraine, either import or export. During the 12 months you have
lived in Ukraine since 1992, you have demonstrated an
understanding of Ukraine, curiosity and determination that has
gained our utmost respect and trust.
    This is an unsalaried position, but it is correct for you
to negotiate whatever commissions and fees you and manufactures
consider appropriate. The EUU invites you to visit Ukraine May,
August, and November 1995 and March, June, September and
December 1996. Every government official will be available for
you to talk to and our private businesses will make every
effort to help you gather information and structure joint
venture contracts. You will be helped in developing positive
and productive business relationships throughout all Ukraine.
    Some of the areas of Ukraine would like to form joint
ventures in include (1) home and building construction (2)
Ukrainian vodka (3) national arts and crafts (4) clothes and
shoes (5) food stuff (6) computers, etc. Ukraine possesses a
market of over 50 million people and can do business in a
market of over 250 million people of Eastern and the
former-Soviet Union.
    This position is, indeed, like representing a country, and
we feel you are the right person to help us as we try to become
a truly capitalistic nation.

    Best regards,

    Vladimir Koutsenko, vice-president
    The Economic Union of Ukraine
    Dnepropetrovsk State University
    72 Gagarin Ave.
    Dnepropetrovsk 320625
    Ukraine

*Letter from the Economic Union of Ukraine, May 30, 1995.*

My father told me that by always being the very best that I can be, I had been preparing myself for this opportunity. In 1979, President Carter, through Mayor Daniel Whitehurst of Fresno, California, awarded me with the award for Outstanding Community Achievement of a Vietnam-era Veteran for my work with people who are disabled, especially brain injured.

The Fresno Veterans of Foreign Wars chapter nominated me for the award. You bet I was honored. I was a 100 percent disabled Vietnam combat veteran who thanked God for my blessings by working with TBI victims around, at that time, Oregon, Washington, and California. I'd had a great job with Weston foods and lost it because of my seizures, and the chances of my ever getting a paying job were slim at best.

I have met many people like me. We have limitations that prevent full-time or even part-time work, but we know we have value and are not afraid of helping people who need us. We thrive on being useful, and no matter what some people think of us, we are proud of ourselves. A young man degraded me in the park one day when I decided that I would try to run and ended up diving into some bushes. Nobody helped me out. When I climbed out, one man told me that that was a stupid thing I had done and told me to get out of the park. He kicked me so hard that my butt was around my throat. I was so anxious that I couldn't talk clearly. He thought I must be drunk and began hitting me before he simply walked away. Four years later, I earned a PhD in psychology and ended up being mentioned in the *Congressional Digest* in a letter that Representative Tony Coelho wrote about me.

This man did not know a thing about me yet beat me up because I was not like he thought I should be. He needed to hurt me to make himself feel better about himself. I felt sorry for him. And I have value! It amazes me that there are people who become defensive merely because a person may seem to look at them the wrong way. I think more of me than that, and I am sure you do too. I think more of you too.

## BACKTRACKING

Going back to the Economic Union of Ukraine, after I returned to the United States, I followed the guidance that was given me and applied for work at a commercial real estate company that had an office in downtown Portland. It was on the top floor of the tall black glass building a couple of blocks from the Civic Auditorium, which was easily the sexiest building in town. When I walked out of there to go to lunch or home, I could feel all the eyes that were surely on me, and I could imagine what the people must be thinking, wondering what kind of work I must do. I loved it and was certain that if they knew, it would blow their minds.

What I did was a dream of almost all the businesspeople I've ever met. After I introduced myself and gave them a copy of a letter from the Economic Union at Ukraine, I was given an office and a telephone and told that if I was doing business, I could call anywhere in the world.

This seemed to be a Russian/Ukrainian business, but I never talked to anyone there, and no one ever talked to me. This felt strange, but I soon discovered that I simply did not have the time for small talk.

## THE CENTER OF THE WORLD

After Ukraine declared its independence from the Soviet Union in November 1991, it came as no surprise to anyone that money from Moscow stopped coming to the millions of people who depended on it. Luckily, people were living in Khrushchev apartments that belonged to the Soviet government. I do not know how some were able to survive— probably from savings or from wages from the Ukrainian government and other sources. But the people survived and seemed willing to help each other. It was a blessing to feel like a part of this.

Complexes where men and women manufactured products that were sent to Moscow attempted to survive, but manufacturing businesses soon had to close their doors. From 1993 to 1995, I met some wonderful people who had almost nothing but would invite me for dinner. They always shared the little that they had. I never saw a poor person on the streets, because they were all poor and did their best to prevent anyone from suffering. To me it was truly amazing and beautiful.

Almost weekly, I made it a point to take up to five of my students to a nice restaurant for dinner. The food was always fantastic, and the restaurant was beautiful. The waiters dressed impeccably and put any

Clark Gable movie to shame. The place I enjoyed taking my students the most was rather large and decorated exceptionally well. I loved everything about it, and my students could not have been more excited. But there was one thing I never got used to. My students and I were always the only customers there.

Talking to a waiter one evening, I learned that the restaurant was always packed until recently. The people had money to spend, and they spent it freely. Dnepropetrovsk had apparently been a closed city, and the people were not allowed to come and go as they pleased. To keep the people happy and not rebellious, the Soviet government built sources of entertainment everywhere. The government needed Dnepropetrovsk to be as much like a paradise as they could make it.

Then when the Russian Ruble stopped coming in, paradise was lost, and everything closed. Almost every factory closed, and I could hear people begging for work. The Communists who once ran Ukraine became the new rich capitalists. The main problem here was "becoming capitalists" who did not become one bit smarter. They did not know what to do.

Meeting with people every day caused me to be aware that Dnepropetrovsk had benefits that other cities in the world could only dream of. For sure, these cities might have some, but no other city in the world has all of them.

Dnepropetrovsk was almost halfway between Asia and Europe. Both markets were huge. The Soviet Union had constructed a magnificent railroad system. And there were so many empty factories available in the city that the government was willing to provide bargains that were so fantastic that almost no one could refuse them. We talked with the city leaders, and they were more than willing to make it possible to redo the factories and put money into the people's pockets. The more we discussed the dream, the more positive we became that we could help make it happen.

We had a population that was almost completely out of work. The more I thought about our goal, the more excited I became. Dnepropetrovsk was a city of nearly one million people, and most of the unemployed population seemed to want to return to work. I talked to unemployed individuals every day, and not a single person I met told me that he would only take a certain type of job. The people I met merely wanted jobs. The physically limited people I met were surprisingly aware that employers would give them jobs they qualified for, and attempting to get a job that only able-bodied people would get might be somewhat unnecessary.

Possibly as important as anything else was the location of Dnepropetrovsk. It was on the Dnepper River, any city planner's dream. The Dnepper River flowed west to Kiev and then up to Belarus. From the south, it went to the Black Sea. Kiev has a fantastic international airport, and rail lines go from Dnepropetrovsk north to Moscow, south to the Black Sea, east to Asia, and west to Europe. For these and other reasons, Dnepropetrovsk is the center of the world, and I wondered how anything could be more obvious.

## THE PERFECT PRODUCT

One thing that impressed me and puzzled me at the same time was that the homebuilders with whom I spent much time practicing Russian (always with Andre my translator to guarantee that I would not miss some things) were building larger homes that only people with extremely healthy incomes could afford. To me this seemed ridiculous and definitely not the way to make the most money. This middle-class population of the world was huge, and no city was in a better place to take advantage of this gigantic source of income. Big homes might sell fairly well, but in comparison to the population that can afford moderately sized homes, the rich would seem like a very small group. My suggestion was to make Dnepropetrovsk the manufactured home center of the world, and I presented this to the Economic Union. I called builders of manufactured homes all over the United States and primarily in Washington and Oregon. What I needed to know was whether they would be willing to relocate part of their businesses to Ukraine.

After telling them I was the United States representative to the Economic Union of Ukraine, I informed them that I could get them the number of factories and warehouses they needed at prices they had never dreamed would be possible. I assumed that they would have a difficult time accepting what I was telling them and, at the same time, I prayed they would be drawn to the possibility of helping a country rebuild itself and become very rich. The world was coming out of a recession, and I could sense that manufactured homes were going to become the next got-to-have product. I asked the Economic Union not to pay me a salary, because it was obvious to me that it could not afford me. My agreement was that I would help set up this empire and could arrange any appropriate commission from the homebuilders. This had nothing to do with my traumatic brain injury. I was not rich then, have never been rich, and could not imagine ever being rich. If I couldn't share my money with the people I cared for, I couldn't see any reason to be rich.

Within a moment, my dreams and the dreams of a nation fell apart. I was viciously attacked, purposely deceived, and sent to a place I never thought existed, even in my worst nightmares. Maybe I will write more about this in the next chapter or possibly in another book. The main thing I want you to be completely sure of is that there is nothing I have ever accomplished that anyone can't accomplish if that person is willing to do what it takes to accomplish her goals. Maybe I could have accomplished my goals all along without the help of anyone else. But why?

Just think of all the ideas from people smarter than I that I would have missed. I know there have been times in my life that I would not listen to criticism that was accurate. What a loss.

What about the times when somebody says something that rings a bell and causes everything to suddenly make sense? I would hate that to happen. I am dense enough, and the idea of allowing myself to be any denser does not impress me.

Nor can I imagine how much more difficult going through life alone would be. If nothing else, the loneliness could be unbearable. Indeed, who likes those lonely moments that sometimes creep up on us for no reason we can think of. Have you ever attempted to carry a heavy package alone?

# Chapter 7

It must be obvious by now that I consider myself just about the most blessed person on earth. Let me change that statement. No matter what the religious image of God may be, if that image is of a caring God who wants the very best for all God's children. In other words, all of God's children are blessed. At the same time, we all have the free will to accept as much of this blessing as we decide we want. Life is not about learning how to live in a sinful world. In reality, it is living in a world that we allow to be a true home for all

the people of the world.

I am blessed to have been torn apart the way I was on May 8, 1967, when my friend Billy Seale and I crashed our helicopter returning from a combat mission in Vietnam. My previous life was taken away in a second, and although I had no idea or awareness of the adventure I would be facing, an entirely new universe was opening up to me. The rotor blade and the metal plate behind my head caused my brain to be shaken in one way and then the next, literally reorganizing the memories of my life until I was without a past.

From then on, everything was a conglomeration of the production of all the emotions a person could possibly experience, and I am so blessed. My brain had to be reorganized, but my brain cells themselves continued the same structural maturity they had before I was injured.

If this had not happened, the creature that I am surely would have died. If God is the universe or is in everything, for some reason that nobody can fully explain, something happened and I was re-created.

I was not re-created perfect, like a superhero, and I make errors and do stupid things like everyone else. I am considered sixty-five because my body is this old. My blank (if you will) brain became aware of the world forty-five years ago. What does this mean? My youngest stepdaughter thinks I'm an old man just because we think differently about just about everything. She looks at me, sees a sixty- five-year-old person, and cannot comprehend that it took me forty- five years of experience in life to get there. Shannon is forty. Am I only five years older than my stepdaughter? Is my beautiful wife twenty-three years older than I am instead of three years older? It must drive Shannon bananas trying to find a single method to interpret age.

This nuttiness is also a blessing. Some people have such an exaggerated perception of what one's age is supposed to mean. When they are young, they are told not to act like a baby. In middle age, they're often told that by whatever age they are, they should know better. At, say, sixty-five, when they act differently than the crowd expects, they might be told to stop being an old man or woman. Something I am told fairly often is, "Don't you ever grow up?" and my response is, "Obviously not, but with your help, I am sure I have no choice." I have a dry sense of humor, but the smile helps me to keep more friends than I lose. I hope.

Can you imagine what a blessing it was that almost all of my first year and a half at Madigan General Hospital, the army hospital in Fort Lewis, were spent in the amputee ward, ward 13? After talking to my mother, who told him I was dying and would not live much longer if they cut off both my legs as they suggested they might have to do, Dr. Marx moved me to the amputee ward in order to experience the stimulation of some brave and determined men. As far as he was concerned, if this did not cause me to want to live, there was no chance I would survive.

As you can tell, it worked even with my being unconscious when they moved me to the amputee ward. He knew my unconscious brain was responding to the loving words and actions shown to me by Kathy and my mother, and he prayed that stimuli from the amputee ward would make me want to continue living. Dr. Marx later told my mother that he had to be truthful. He did not think this would do the trick, but he did not know what else to do to have any chance of helping me be "born again."

My entire life since then has been one blessing after another. I am also convinced that Jim's life had been no different, but I cannot talk about that, because he died before I was born. Can you imagine what a blessing it was that I was still in a body cast and unable to experience too much around me when I regained consciousness? If I had experienced too much stimulation too quickly, there is a possibility that my brain would not have been able to coordinate all these new messages, which could have prevented the appropriate coordinating of future messages.

Why did God want me in ward 13? These men had the guts to live, and God wanted me to be like them as much as I could possibly be. In 1967, traditional psychology and psychiatry/medicine universally felt that people with brain injuries as severe as mine suffered and then died or ended up being vegetables for whatever time they had left. Dr. Marx felt that way also, but my mother's faith made him want to believe that he could help me survive. The men in ward 13 were with me every waking hour. They knew how to help me because they knew how they would want to be treated if they were as helpless as I was. The way they treated me did not come from a book. It came from their hearts. When Kathy and her parents, Jeannine and Vernon E. Euston, as well as my family came to visit me on weekends, my ward mates would stand back and listen to them compliment me for all the things I'd learned to do since their last visit.

My ward mates and the nurses knew why I learned so many new things. They had taught me everything I learned. I could not score high enough on the IQ test to stay in the army, and the chances were very slim that I had the "brains" to decide what I needed to learn and teach myself. I was so very blessed that God made it possible for some people to show me real caring and concern even though we had never met. They did not have to treat me as well as they did, but a positive feeling came over them that made them want me to know that they were part of my life. There was the bus driver who carried me from my wheelchair onto the bus, and who, with tears in his eyes, said thank you. There was the woman near my parents' Madison Street home who, after seeing me try to walk with my walker, rushed out of her home and gave me a hug. She too was crying. I will never forget the female student at Mt. Hood Community College who made an effort to be my friend when some other students (not all) would ignore me for their own reasons. I think she became a respiratory therapist and married a respiratory therapist in Portland. She was a truly beautiful person who cared for people, like me, and I will never forget her.

If we cannot see the caring people in this world, it is because we do not look. It is that simple. I looked for caring people. I will always need them in my life. I cherish knowing that they exist. If we do not care whether these beautiful people exist, it is usually because some part of us fears that when we need someone, nobody will be there for us. For some of us, it is like our belief in God. We are afraid that we will devote all of our time and energy to something that does not exist.

During the past forty-five years, doctors have told me four times that I am going to die. The last time was three years ago, when the Veterans Administration doctor told me that I was going to die if I didn't take a certain medication. She and another doctor told us this after my wife and I came in for a visit. I had my own reasons and told her that if it meant going back to being like a zombie I would rather take my chances. I might be stupid, but, yes, I am willing to take my chances.

As my mother taught me, it is difficult to feel as if you do not have enough or that you deserve more when you feel so blessed and grateful for what you have. I have been a mental health counselor to help people in need and have done my best to help them get what they need. On the other hand, I have met people who are so negative about life that they seem determined not to be likable, not to be healthy or happy, and not to even consider helping anyone else. These people, with no idea how to better their lives, do exist, and as they drag themselves down, they drag down the people around them. This is so sad. We have all seen sad or tragic situations that we wish had never happened, and we do whatever we can to help. Most of the situations are ones that people do not realize they helped cause, and they have no idea how they can help correct them.

Psychologists cannot do everything. If I do not actually want something to happen and am not willing to do anything I can to solve a problem, it simply is not going to happen. Even though I have done some foolish things that have not helped me one bit, for most of my life I've tried to get counseling from a psychologist. Sometimes a close friend or my wife can be just as helpful. My blessings have been knowing that I need help and being able to get help. Much of the help I have received has helped me help other people. No two people in the world ever have exactly the same problem, but sometimes the help I have gotten is similar enough to what another needs that I have an idea what may help that person.

I am selective with whom I try to make friends. Not all people want me to be a friend; this is life. We are all different. Still, it is my professional and personal opinion that unless you are perfect and can make it through life alone, having friends is a good way to go. I remember a client who blurted out, "Dr. Meade, you know everything, and I'm so glad you are my therapist." Our next three sessions were devoted to helping the person understand and accept that he might be projecting onto me his feelings that he wants to feel about himself. He knew my medical history, and I had to explain that everything, not some things, not most things, but everything I know, someone else has taught me. This is true for everyone. Being a hermit in our social world is like telling yourself that you do not want to learn anymore. If you stop learning in a social world, you start being worthless. In the eyes of God, everyone has value, and believing that you have no value is the unwillingness (out of fear) to be the person God wants you to be. My life is a blessing, and even if we never meet, I thank you for being part of my life.

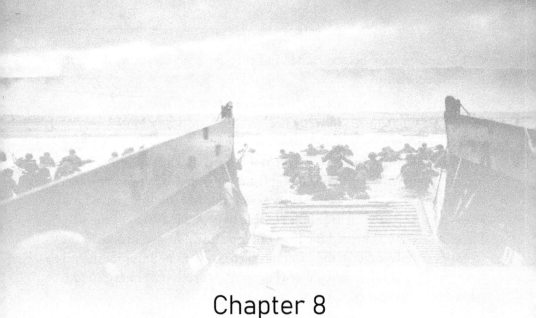

# Chapter 8

### FROM A PILOT TO AN ANIMAL TO A PHD—SOME HISTORY

This may sound a bit self-centered, but I have been concerned with my mental state since I became aware that there is such a thing. He did not mean to hurt me, but my father seemed to say almost every time we met, "You used to have such a beautiful brain." I did not know what he meant and used to wonder what kind of a compliment this was—or if it was. What used to amaze me was that for several years, I could memorize almost an entire book or paper and, while remembering the words, have no idea of the meaning of what I had read. How could I remember the words, even in appropriate order, and not the meaning of what I was reading?

After three semesters of nontransferable classes, sometimes called bonehead classes, at Mt. Hood Community College, I took a semester of psychology, sociology, and political science. On my first exam in sociology, I earned an A, which amazed the teacher. What amazed him was that my answers were almost word for word as written in the book. He did not accuse me of cheating but wanted to know how I was able to do this. I almost never spoke in class, which led him to believe I probably could not keep up with the class. He knew that I could not print quickly and stayed with me for the extra time he allowed me to complete the exam. I never looked up from my paper, and he probably figured that if I was cheating, I'd invented some way that was different from anything he could imagine.

What I told him was that I had memorized the book. How could I do this? I'd told myself that I was going to remember the entire book, and I did. Thinking about what I had done, I wondered why I could memorize a book and learn so little. (I cannot remember what it was like to know anything, but at the same time, I knew what it was to be confused by everything that took place or occurred around me and remembered what I was confused by. It would baffle me that a fly was so small, and as I watched the flies around me, I would wonder what they were thinking. I remember once asking Squeak what flies think, and when my brother told me that they don't, I recall thinking, *That's stupid; how do they expect to know where they are going?*

My sociology lecturer thought I was some kind of a weird genius, and my brother must've been sure that I was on some kind of cloud, not knowing where I was going and just drifting along. Years later, at Portland State University, my psychology professor was passing around the class a copy of the short test of the intelligence quotient. I had taken it five years earlier when, the psychologist at Madigan General Hospital asked me questions. I could not answer a single question. But after five years, I could write down the ten questions before the test ever reached me.

After being conscious for forty-five years, I cannot do that on a bet. Today if I set out to memorize a book or pamphlet, by the time I got halfway through it, I probably would forget what the first half was all about. A doctor friend of mine told me a few years ago that when I woke up, because I did not know anything, there was massive room for new memories of every kind … for new brain cells. This made sense to me. He went on to explain that the reason I do not know much nonsensical information is that I never learned it. The reason I never learned what the average person learns the first eighteen years of life is that for me, those years never existed. What makes me feel better is the possibility that if my brain cannot store much new information, it can make sense out of old information. That would be good.

My entire life has been so much better than simply good. It has been great. But believe me, I have had my moments. I don't even mind sharing them. I finally figured out, in the end, that I cause all my own problems. Somebody may do something that does not do me any favors but causes me problems instead, and I am the person who has the obligation of dealing with the issue in a way that is best for me and the people around me.

Obviously, I have spent my life working with brain-injured individuals and their families, and I have seen many people who probably were as injured as I was when I returned from Vietnam. I have never diagnosed the severity of any brain injury beyond the definitions of any degree of injury.

I returned from Vietnam unconscious and began to respond without being aware of what was happening in my surroundings, acting like a vicious animal and attacking and growling at whatever was around me. When Ed Rudy growled at people and tried to bite them, he was responding to his inability to communicate. Similarly, I did not want anyone in my space and would try to attack whoever was near me.

My life was as if I were traveling up the evolutionary tree, and some of the segments I passed through seemed so obvious. A psychologist tried to explain that what I had seemingly done was grow on the evolutionary tree, and I was not like people who had never had their brains literally reorganized.

But why did my brain functionally evolve? Note that I did not say *heal*—it *evolved*. Whatever God is, I truly believe that everything worked together so perfectly that even with no brain cells coordinated in a way that would fit together perfectly, every new experience or memory was accepted and continued to form new connections. Every neuroscientist knows that cells that do not seem compatible do not join together. I was simply blessed.

Every living human being is a perfect coordination of brain cells that must work together perfectly. If this were not so, the misconstrued being would fall apart and cease to exist. When any person says that he is less than anyone else, what he is saying is that somehow his over fifty billion brain cells do not fit together well—that they are out of whack, and consequently he is lacking. Why do people put themselves down like that? A brain that is lacking information can gain the information (new cells) like anyone else, through practice. I've met people in college who flunked out because they did not study and people who never got into college because they did not take the time or make the effort to know what they needed to know to be accepted.

Being smarter or dumber than anyone else has nothing to do with anything. What most people think is that being smart is actually being informed. The actual reason a person is lacking in being informed is often because the person is not making the attempt to become informed. No one is born with the knowledge that is available from his surroundings. We are all born equal, at least in this way. (I stopped comparing myself to Prince Philip long ago).

I have a friend who decided several years ago to become a registered nurse. She was already a licensed practical nurse with over twenty years of experience and information that was ingrained over the years just from doing the same things repeatedly. Most of the people who entered the registered nursing program were young people with no experience, and she knew that she would be helping some of them. She mentioned that she had attempted the program before and was not successful, but this time, she was going to make it. She went as far as emphasizing that she had gotten a D in chemistry and As, Bs, and Cs in other courses at a nearby community college.

Then one day, she told me that she had dropped out of the nursing program. It took me completely by surprise. What she told me was that she was not as smart as the younger students. She felt it was a certainty that she had forgotten all she needed to know. In her mind, she was destined to fail.

Over the years, I have talked to dozens of people who had convinced themselves that they were lacking the intelligence other people had to be successful or complete projects. What is so unfortunate is that people claim the right to certify or reject another person's or their own intelligence without any legitimate evidence. At one time, even the most successful professors were telling us that a person's intelligence does not change. Today, after years of denying the reality, they realize that a healthy person can learn well into advancing years. This is termed plasticity, and I will discuss this in another book.

The main thing I need to stress, putting all I have said together, is very simple. Nothing you have done limits what you can do. Being smart is different from being knowledgeable, and if you want to, you can make yourself more knowledgeable by simply going to a community college or trying an online program. I remember my own father saying, "I am too old to learn something new." We know now that for a healthy person, this just isn't t so. More people are continuing their educations at ages that were once unheard of. The reasons that people once used to convince others or themselves that they could not or should not try something no longer exist.

Again, the times I growled at Kathy and my mother due to my brain injury, I was like an animal protecting itself. They have told me that they feared I would die, but they did fear that I might never get better. They were members of the same society as the rest of us and could only know what they were told or read. In 1967, they were led to believe that, if I lived, I lived, and if I died, I died. They were also told rather emphatically that a brain-injured person does not get better. The best they could hope for was for me to linger before I died. Unbelievably, I never have been given and the reason I stopped responding to anything and went into a completely vegetative state. Dr. Marx transferred me to ward 13, but the medical profession did not change its opinion. I was a hopeless case.

When I entered a vegetative state, they were willing to let me go if God called me. They had seen me suffer for so long that my parents wondered if they were being selfish by hanging on. They were not willing to accept my dying if they could do anything to help me live. Some smart people were telling them that my chance of living was ten thousand to one. Kathy and my mother were with me up to twenty-four hours a day and ignored such talk. And when I regained consciousness, a new world awakened. I am no more a hero than anyone I have ever met and have been cowardly as much as anyone. I will never think that I am less than anyone or not try something because I think somebody is better than I am. My assumption is that I am just as good as anyone, not a single bit better but the same.

My PhD in psychology is the tool God used to prove to me that a perfect and universal God has put my brain back together, which human experts openly admitted that they had no idea how to do. After reading book after book on how to be a truly functional human being, I've had to conclude that none of these books in any way apply to a case as violent as mine. The Supreme Being that has redone billions of years of evolution to create the person I am is the perfect God that I have chosen to worship. God has not allowed nature to reform a super brain. What God has done is re-create a human brain perfectly, without error. God was the guidebook and permitted elements to work together and become a workable brain.

I have prayed for God to heal my other physical limitations. This might be considered a weakness on my part, but I can be embarrassed by my occasional poor speech. Sometimes I attempt to overcompensate for the excessive energy it takes me to talk clearly, making a complete jerk of myself. I cannot feel the skin below the knee of my left leg, which is completely numb. In other words, if I had not seen it for forty-five years, I would not know it existed. Some people think I have a difficult time going down steps because of the pain in my knee, which sometimes feels as if a knife is going through it. The truth is that going down the steps with a leg you cannot feel is one of the most bizarre sensations you ever want to experience. I am not saying this simply because I'm a weakling.

Back to my PhD. As I have already mentioned, I was working as a sales representative for Hunt-Wesson Foods in the Willamette Valley of Oregon, a great job and a great company. My seizures caused by my head injury returned big time, and Hunt-Wesson had to put me on a medical leave of absence. I had gone through violent periods of epileptic seizures (status epilepticus) and nearly died. I felt confident that the Veterans Administration had done this for other veterans, and that I wasn't anybody special when the VA called and asked me if I wanted to go to California and earn my PhD. I have never told this to anyone, but I started to cry. God had blessed me so very much indeed every day of this new life, and I tried to learn to act like a human being but failed God so many times. I did not understand. Just the same, in my heart, I knew this was a blessing from God. Even though I didn't even have a master's degree, I knew that God would make me as ready as I needed to be. On a couple of occasions, I told myself that I was not the person for this adventure because I am severely brain injured, and severely brain-injured people do not earn PhDs.

I finally realized that my fears and doubts were leading me to give up on this opportunity. Part of me wanted to earn a PhD, and the other part of me was telling me that I would only fail so there was no point in trying. I needed to talk to someone. Talking to myself was not doing me any good. I even went as far as thanking God for the blessing of this fantastic opportunity to learn to be an even better counselor to the people who needed me, but I told him that I was the wrong guy. I reminded God of my medical history and felt convinced that this would set things straight.

I finally knew what I had to do. I had said hello to a Christian psychologist but had never actually spoken to him. He seemed like a nice man, and I asked him if he could take a few moments to help me deal with a blessing from God. His response caught me completely by surprise. Although I was expecting him to say no or give me a telephone number to call to set up an appointment, he told me that he had about thirty minutes left to speak and would meet with me as soon as he was finished. I was completely shocked, and as soon as he walked away, I started making faces like tears were in my eyes.

When he returned, I confessed that when I asked him for a meeting I completely forgot that I had been listening to him for an hour. He laughed and joked," I sometimes have that influence on people." I told him that I had heard him before and found him to be a great Christian psychologist. I told him that my issue was constantly on my mind and that I needed his help. After I told him about my problem, the first thing he asked was, "Do you believe this is a blessing from God—you know how some people convince themselves that God is leading them in one way or another yet God has nothing to do with it?" I told him that I wanted to believe that it was a blessing from God, but I simply had a hard time accepting that God picked the right guy. He asked me why I felt this, and I responded, "I did not think I knew enough to attend a graduate school to earn a PhD in psychology. My patients will know I am stupid."

Then he told me that if all the cases he heard during the day were as easy as mine, he would have enough time to take a second job. I had shown him my problem after about two questions. "Okay," he said calmly, "you told me that you believe that God blessed you with this offer to move to California and earn a PhD. You would be paid to earn your PhD. The VA would pay for all your books. Is that what you said?" After I said yes, he continued. "You had a super high GPA in college. School boards are pretty good at this, and if they accept you, this most likely means that the board feels you are as good as they have ever accepted." He was quiet for a moment and looked over his notes. Then he went on: "Have I missed something that makes this less than a perfect offer?"

"That's the problem," I replied. "It is too perfect, and I don't know if I can do my part."

"That's the problem," he answered fairly quickly. "You answered it yourself. You know it is a blessing from God, and you're afraid you will let them down."

"That's what I've been telling you," I responded.

"Okay," he said. "God knows your past and wants to bless you with another chance. That means God has forgiven you and knows you are good enough to succeed. He's showing you by offering an opportunity very few people in the world will ever have. What you have to realize is that our perfect God knows that people assume things, and God knows that you are the person. It is up to you to realize that you are not as smart as God, and God is telling you that you are God's number one choice for this in the entire country, the entire universe."

What I finally realized was that God offers this free choice. We do not have to do what God offers us. What God is saying is that we are good enough to try and that we can do anything we want to accomplish *if* we are willing to do what it takes to accomplish our goals. Saying we cannot do something only means that we are not willing to do whatever it takes to accomplish our goals. Sometimes it is not the right time. Sometimes other obligations are more important. There are a zillion reasons for not wanting to do or accomplish things. Unless the reasons are something you cannot control or that you have not learned to deal with yet, "I can't" is not a reason. (Again, other people told me that I would be an idiot if I did not accept this invitation.)

I know what it is like to be held back by a situation you cannot control—or at least feel you cannot control. I'm also going to add something that you will not hear very often: Sometimes, if you truly believe that you are unable to make an effort to do something, in reality, you are unable to make the effort. If you are scared and think you will, I pray that the opportunity will come again and you will make the effort you need to make to be successful. If you do not experience this drive, I pray for you just the same and hope that you are happy with yourself, which is most important.

Yes, I made an effort to be like my ward mates. They were all my brothers, and I wanted them to be proud of my accomplishments. This made me happy. That is why I would do anything, as it made me feel good about myself. What someone else may feel influences the humanness I claim, but I make the decisions about it. Some things make my wife very happy, and I try to do things that help her be happy. It is my decision to do things that cause her to feel good. Then she decides to be happy or not. I cannot make her happy. Nobody can make another person happy. Still, if what I do helps her feel happy, I have a good reason to feel happy. I love to do things that make her and others want to be happy. Believe me, this was not always the case.

I started feeling self-conscious and negative after I left the hospital. Even though I've known many wonderful people, I have also frequently felt more abandoned and lonelier than I thought I could ever feel. People I'd thought were close friends decided that it was not worth their time and effort to see me or say anything to me. My brother, a certified mental health counselor, discussed my feelings of abandonment several years ago, and he said something I did not expect him to say to his big brother. He said it with deep concern, but like many people who came to see me, I wanted him to take away my problem and make everything fantastic again. This is what he told me: "James, I cannot take away your problem. If you are lonely and feel abandoned at times, would you agree that this is something *you* have the power to deal with?"

One of his questions was this: "What do I do when I lose anything?" This was a no-brainer. What does anyone do when he loses anything? He gets something to replace what he's lost. Others decide they're going to hide from the world and mope around. I have a difficult time seeing any joy in this, but I have met some people who feel some sort of gain from suffering. What my brother told me was a reminder of a truth that I have seen more times than I can count. Making friends needs to be a priority for every disabled person. This should be true for most people, but for us, friends add more to our lives than most people can imagine.

I have admitted that at times I felt lonely and abandoned, and I can recall times when talking with a friend or friends had been so important in helping me. Even more important actually, friends helped me experience conversations that caused me to feel so good that all I realized was completeness and joy. These times create memories that seem to come to my awareness whenever I need them. Yes, when I want to feel good, I bring up memories that I know will be good for me. When I have a question that is troubling me, I call someone I trust to help me. Some people are choosy regarding what they will help me deal with. This may sound small on my part, but as much as I care about their welfare, these people are not the people I know will be there when I need them; they are not my close friends.

All people are different, and we feel more inclined to be friends with some people than others. As much as we might question this, there are many people we feel compatible with, and people who are most compatible tend to have lasting friendships and make themselves available for friendship. People do not typically shun disabled people because they hate us or fear us. Instead, they simply do not know how to act around us and are afraid they will insult us in some way. Many people want to be friends but simply do not know where to start. And yes, there are some people I don't want as friends. On the other hand, I cherish the opportunity to try to find people who are willing to be friends.

When my ward mates at Madigan General Hospital went home to their families in the western United States, I felt more than a little disoriented. I was not afraid, but besides my family, I had no friends. I missed the closeness and trust I had with my ward mates, and this world I now lived in was completely new to me.

In my world, I did not know where I came from and even wondered if I came from anywhere. The first world I had ever known was ward

13, and regardless of where I was, my world was never larger than what I could see. When traveling on the Greyhound bus to Portland from Madigan, I could not see scenes long enough to remember them. I would not forget them but simply was not able to incorporate them as anything I could comprehend later.

Just as we see what we expect to see, I could not remember what I could not imagine existed. My mental images of the world I found myself in were as unclear as my confusion caused them to be. Nothing made sense to me because I had no reality to base anything on.

When I attempt to recall my memories of some of my past, a picture of my reality is like a kaleidoscope of colors and images because I am clearly remembering the total confusion. This is what complete confusion looks like, and what I see in my memory, in all its bizarreness, is all that it can be.

I needed people to help me realize I truly existed. For years, I would sometimes feel that I was in a dream. I enjoyed the people in this dream and was willing to live in it. Without a past, I could not imagine a future. And I did not know what one needs to know to be scared. Despite all I have experienced, not knowing enough to be scared had to have been a blessing from God. Meeting all the people who guided me to be the person I am today was another blessing. I would not have survived without both of these blessings.

As far as being alone, I love my wife but have times when I simply feel I need to be alone. The opposite of this is the need for fellowship and interacting with people, which can add the energy we need to accomplish so many goals. Talking to people you trust can present options you never thought of and can help you find answers you simply want from another opinion from someone you respect and sometimes you merely help to expand your mind. Talking to someone you feel likes you often tends to increase 's self-esteem and self-confidence.

Some people tell me, "I know you are a PhD in psychology because you ask so many questions.' I'm not sure this is always meant to be a compliment, but I have been asking questions on just about anything for as long as I can remember. This is how we learn as children, and I have been blessed to have another opportunity to learn about living when I was twenty. Yes, I am sixty-five and have had forty-five years to get there.

So ultimately, I feel that we need friends. At Madigan, my ward mates were constantly helping me in any way they possibly could, and somebody was always with me at home. At the VA hospital, I was a Vietnam veteran helicopter pilot who could not remember his past, and other veterans were always asking me if I needed any help.

Maybe you can imagine what it was like when there were not any people I knew or people who knew me. Even in a wheelchair, I liked to go around the VA hospital to places I had never seen before, and not being able to perceive how far I had gone from my ward, I would look around and realize that I had no idea where I was. Anywhere I was that I could not see my ward was like another world to me. For some reason, almost all the orderlies I asked to help me knew who this lost veteran who was always lost was, and because of their kindness, I was never alone very long. They were kind to me, and I knew that every orderly and nurse was my friend—and friends do not let friends down.

# Chapter 9

## HOW IT WAS EXPLAINED TO ME

**M**y second closest friend in the world (after my brother David) once described things as "typical James Meade Jr." I do not remember my first semester of college psychology, which I took before joining the army, and I have no idea what my second semester was about. Nothing made any sense to me, and I decided to memorize the textbook. As I recall, Pat Laury, my counselor, taught the class, and our class discussions helped me visualize what I had memorized. I took second semester psychology, sociology, and political science from Betty Roberts and memorized all three textbooks as best I could.

My methods for passing the courses were definitely different from any other student's, but I earned Bs in all three courses and was accepted to enter Portland State University in Portland, Oregon, where I did exceptionally well and completed college with a 3.53 GPA. I do not remember the professor of the class by name, but he and I were talking before class about what had happened to my brain when the helicopter rotor blade struck me in the head and the possible reason I had regained my intelligence so quickly despite having no cognitive rehabilitation. He told me that my history was too far out to make sense even to him, and nothing he had been taught in his studies could explain it. He couldn't explain why my head had not been completely cut off when the helicopter rotor blade struck me so hard that my head knocked back my bolted-down seat. I have been told repeatedly that I am the only person who has ever survived such a striking.

## WIPE OUT

My professor said that there was no chance he would even think about what he would have said if I were not sitting across his desk from him, and he was not fairly sure I was not a ghost. He was going to accept the *Reader's Digest* article he read as truthful (since it *is* the *Reader's Digest*), but everything he knew about the brain convinced him that I was dead and merely haven't figured it out yet.

When the rotor blade struck me, it violently knocked my head into the metal plate that protected the back of my head from bullets. When the blade struck my head, my brain cells were forced toward the back of my head. When the cells hit the back of my skull, it was coup-contrecoup, which in itself could have killed me or caused a severe brain injury.

In my case, the coup-contrecoup was greatly exaggerated when my head slammed into the plate, which could have caused every cell in my brain to be disorganized, and this caused neuropathy and my brain to no longer carry the same message and response that it once did. This is a bit beyond forgetting my past. With the messages in the neural pathways of my brain gone, it is as if they never existed. My brain was completely blank. This is still difficult for me to imagine. I have no memory of my past and only a memory of what I've been told. Still, I cannot envision what it must have been like to have neurons mostly displaced. I do not know what to think of the ten- week period of "sleep" I experienced.

## BEGINNING AGAIN

Looking back forty-five years, my mother has had a difficult time accepting that what she watched me experience and helped me grow through was real and not from a horror story. According to my mother, she saw me try and fail at practically everything I attempted, but then I'd try some more. The *Reader's Digest* article about me mentioned my trying to learn to walk on parallel bars, falling, getting up and trying to walk, falling and getting up ... over and over again. When I was too exhausted to pull myself up, I would crawl up and down the parallel bars and continue until I could not do that any longer. I remember trying to button my shirt repeatedly until a ward mate told me to give it a break until tomorrow, when I could try again, and he would help me button my shirt. Karen, my physical therapist at Madigan invited me to the staff cafeteria for lunch, but long before that, I had given up trying to learn to eat without throwing food all over the place, and at lunch with her, I did not eat anything. This embarrassed me because I wanted to eat with other people instead of by myself on my bed. After all these years, I still do not have the manual flexibility that will allow me to type on the computer or write quickly. But I can feed myself fairly well. There was not anything I did not have to learn, exactly as when I was a child, and when the doctors told my parents that they did not know what else they should do to help me, my parents decided that they were going to teach me exactly as they had when I was a child. They were going to start from the beginning and work up from there.

## SOCIAL RULES

From what I was told, despite being message-free, my brain cells had mature structure. I am not a cell biologist and don't know exactly what mature structure means. However, from what I recall reading, cells team up with other cells they are compatible with, and my newly blank neural pathways were bombarded with new messages that took up spaces that my brain injury created.

Social rules and standards of behavior can be the most difficult for anyone to learn. They often change what may seem to be a logical reason, and they are often culturally decided in a multicultural society that cannot explain them fully. At the same time, punishments for violations and rewards for positive behaviors can fluctuate in degree, from exaggerations to complete disregard.

Some people are considered stupid because they cannot say or do what is considered appropriate. I was a social idiot. I did not have the opportunity to learn preferred social behavior, which was rather impossible since I was in the hospital, and what I did not know, I simply did not know. One example would be my kissing hostesses on the cheek when I said good night. Everything I was learning about social life was learned from early-era television programs, and in the ones I watched, the hostess of a dinner or gathering was always given a kiss good night as a guest left. As far as I was aware, this is what you did.

My brother accompanied me to parties, and he one day told me that this was not appropriate behavior, especially when I had never met the hostess before. He had never told me that before, and I felt like a complete jerk. I did not know what to do and started crying. I had worked so hard to be socially acceptable, and I had failed, a pain I did not know how to deal with. (Although you can bet this was the last hostess I ever kissed good-bye.)

I think I mentioned several pages back that even after working with Karen, my physical therapy nurse, for about six months, I still had not learned to walk without support. As hard as I tried, I simply could not maintain my balance well enough to take more than one step. I finally learned to crawl, but even that took a while. The problem was not my leg. I lived on the amputee ward, and nobody ever told me that it was unusual not to feel my left leg below my knee. It was as if it did not exist. I never mentioned this to my doctor or Karen, and they never knew that I could not feel my left leg. I would put my right leg out to take a step and do just fine. Whereas most people would then bring the left leg forward, my upper body would lean forward, my left leg would remain motionless, and I would fall on my face with no idea why, promising myself that I would keep trying as long as I needed to.

Even today, going down steps can be a bit tricky, but walking in general is no problem. I think about all the things I can do rather than about all the trouble I had learning to do them. I can do things that even professionals once thought I would never be able to do. Life has not always been easy, and there are incidences I would not repeat for anything. All my failures finally led to victories, and most of all, I learned to like myself. Instead of feeling like a nobody because of my failures, I realized that trying was just as important as being a success. I could feel the respect that my efforts for creating and decided this was what I wanted. Winners are people who do their best. If a person stops trying, he is soon forgotten, while people never stop cheering for the ones who continue to make the effort.

## Failure Is Not Necessarily a Loss

Because of my history, I am often called a winner, and I often hear about all that I have accomplished. I acknowledge these compliments because they make me feel good, and they are the support that I need to help me continue efforts that challenge my determination to go on.

Have I accomplished all the heroic efforts that people who hear these compliments may assume? The people who praise me so loudly know, or need to know, that I have accomplished a lot, but I have failed a tremendous amount more … I cannot count the number of times that I have started efforts that I decided were not worth continuing to try to accomplish.

I am not ashamed of this. Yes, I have had times when I wondered if I was being one of those quitters that so many people enjoy singling out. I can imagine being called a coward and know that it would hurt. Simply hearing a derogatory name in one's mind can cause a person to continue even when he should not.

There are times when even efforts that once seemed so productive or were bound for success clearly revealed that they may not be the dreams one once thought they surely were. Some realities merely change. It is not your fault or my fault or anyone's fault. It simply happens sometimes.

Some of us are disabled. I do not know anyone who tells himself, "When I grow up, I am going to be disabled." It merely happens.

I am told that I loved to fly and loved the guys I flew with. Flying helicopters is exciting, and flying helicopters in combat is more exciting. I have heard this more times than I can remember. My parents have many letters from me where I stressed that I had the best job in the world. I also wanted them to know that if I was shot down and I died, I was doing what I loved and felt proud of what I was doing.

Then one day I woke up not knowing anything. I was in a complete body cast and did not know enough to suspect that this was unusual. In the last thirty-five-plus years of talking to brain-injured and other disabled people I have heard similar stories hundreds of times: "I woke up not knowing where I was or how I had gotten there." Like me, they had not planned the incident that would change their lives.

When Billy Seale and I lifted off earlier that day, we expected to return that evening in good shape, but sometimes war changes plans. Every disabled person I have ever talked to has seen his plan abruptly changed.

Everything changes. My having no past is different from most people, but I know I cannot function like most people, and I also know that I have to make special efforts to accomplish what they do automatically.

Yes, I have learned to behave in ways that overcome much of my disability or at least conceal it, and I have found alternate ways to accomplish things that I could not have otherwise.

It truly saddens me that I have met many people who are ashamed and angry that they cannot do things they could before their injury or disease. What is there to be mad about? In most of these cases, I feel almost certain that their anger is often displaced jealousy. If they developed unique ways to accomplish things, they would have no reason to feel jealous or angry.

My left leg is slightly shorter than my right leg. This is easy; I wear a lift in my left shoe. I have never been fully able to use a fork; I use a spoon. I have trouble going up stairs; I always use the railing. I cannot drive a car; what is so shameful about riding a bus or taking a taxi … or walking? I cannot run. This is another easy one; I do not need to try to run.

I do not have the coordination in my hands to write clearly, except uncomfortably slowly. I print. For the same reason, I do not type. Evelyn usually types for me and uses the computer to find information for me. During some evenings, especially when it's late evening, my speech can be chancy. I never go out late and usually plan to be home by about eight or nine o'clock. My leg, hip, and back can cause me extreme pain at night. Of course, I must take pain medication every day and have a comfortable bed that is warm during the winter.

I cannot taste or smell. Of course, I do not know what anything smells or tastes like, but I have to be careful that I do not keep food long enough so that is spoils. I hear often that people love the fresh air, and I wish I could experience it also. I love to take my wife to restaurants, and I love having great conversations in a restaurant environment.

Years ago, my VA doctors told me to stay away from the stove because I can burn my hand and not feel it. I use our microwave.

Since nobody can find a cure for my posttraumatic seizures (epilepsy), I do my best to prevent or stay away from stressful situations, and I would love to be able to get eight fantastic hours of sleep every night. My left leg below my knee has been numb for over forty-five years. When I regained consciousness, I did not know I had legs, and when the doctor removed the body cast, I saw my leg, but because I could not feel it, it was as if it never existed. Living with a leg I cannot feel is an annoyance, but long ago, I determined that I would never let it get me down. It takes a conscious effort to command my leg to do anything, but after all these years, I do what I need to do almost automatically.

Most of the people who see me have no idea I am rated 100 percent disabled or have any limitations. I thank God that I have so many physical limitations, for my condition gives me some understanding of what the individuals I work with are going through, and to me, this is a true blessing.

# Chapter 10

I have read books by many mental health professionals who state that many people are usually friendly to other people because it is part of their nature. This is one of the most general comments I have ever read, and I think I support it. I feel reluctant to comment but would be comfortable saying that people generally like people who are like themselves rather than people who are not like them. There are exceptions, of course, but I have never met anyone who preferred to be with people who did not have standards and needs and interests that were at least similar.

I once brought this question up with associates, and it amazed me that possibly a good one-third of the people I talked to said that they liked and preferred to be friends with people who were different from them. Forgive me, but although these people said that, it does not seem like reality.

People who know me don't have to hate me or not want to be my friend. I like many people that I do not especially enjoy being around more than casually. At the same time, if someone includes me in his don't-need-to-see-him-more-than-necessary list of acquaintances, I am not offended. There is a good chance that we are different enough that he is on my list too.

My wife tells me that she is amazed that I will talk to anyone I meet. If the truth be known, she has this a wee bit wrong. I love to talk with people who are not mean to other people and who are considerate of the feelings and welfare of others. I will talk about anything with anyone, but these are my standards from which I will not waiver. If we speak from two different understandings but can still follow these rules, our talks can be all the more enjoyable. The key is mutual respect, acceptance, and willingness to learn.

The way my wife describes me is probably quite accurate. I like to think so. I also like to think that I (and people like me) make this world a better place for all of us. Still, I cannot deny that many friends have been with me during these discussions and could not believe what they were hearing. They could not believe that I would/could honor the existence of beliefs that were so different from what *we* believe.

Being truthful, the way they would describe the people I had these discussions with often left me with the impression that they were more opposed to the people I felt honored to share ideas with than what they were saying. My father knew some people he considered friends for life, but he would also have discussions with anyone who was willing to accept the same rules I insist on: respect, acceptance, and willingness to learn.

It seems possible that most people want to live in peace, but it also seems that most (yes, *most*) people think that the only way peace can occur is if our opponents feel exactly like *us*. Most people also seem to believe that the truest and most perfect form of democracy is our own.

I need to talk to people every day in order to maintain my ability to talk, and the people who are willing to talk to me are indeed doing me a blessing. If they are willing to talk to me and answer all my questions, as far as I am concerned, they have earned my respect. I honor their positions and views.

If this seems single-directed, I will admit that some of the discussions I have had seem to start and end this way: I will say something, and all the person I am trying to discuss things with does is argue against my points without trying to learn more about what I am saying. Or the person may argue his interests and refuse to discuss the possible merits of mine.

I have some views that I hold to dearly, for they are part of the person I am. Still, there is nothing I think I know that could not be wrong, and if someone else has a different view about something, so be it.

Do you ever think about the positive impact that we could have on the world by listening to the world? We can let the people know that the rules of communication demand that we listen with respect, ask questions, and share our opinions. In my opinion, there is no way we would not be helping our world become be a better place. We need to ask respectful questions, for knowing why anyone feels the way he does is equally as important as knowing what he does.

# Chapter 11

**W**hat can I do to be all I can be? How do I decide what I should do?

I would like to believe that most people decide for themselves what school or college they are going to apply to, what they are going to study, what they plan on doing for the rest of their lives, and other decisions they need to make. There's no doubt that many people have different opinions about how a person should respond to just about anything, and making any decision that will affect the rest of one's life has to be somewhat frightening.

Any decision of this sort that will affect the rest of one's life will be one that a person will likely lose sleep over, and the person who does not realize the many factors necessary to determine what seems the best decision is more than a little naive, lacking information that is essential to know.

What are you interested in? How does what I am interested in apply to what I will want out of life? I think it might also be important to consider why you are interested in some things and not other things. We all have priorities that exist because they are fun or because of the constant contact we can have with friends, but we sometimes need to separate immediate pleasure from what might have the greatest long-term rewards.

Along similar lines, what am I most willing to dedicate myself to learning and taking the time to master? Different people reach the point where they can make this decision at different times in their lives, and some people experience things that prevent them from planning the distant future. Until a person can make a final decision, he needs to research all possibilities that present themselves. Decisions change, and making a decision should not have to be a life-or-death situation. Winners continue to be open their entire lives and take the time and make the effort to learn what can add to their lives in a positive way while also adding to the lives of others.

This does not mean going from job to job. The winner learns to do his job as well as anyone else possibly could while also learning to help others be as happy and fulfilled as they can possibly be. This individual does his best and remains dedicated to an effort until the task is done. This person's self-respect is healthy, and he dedicates his life to helping other people better their lives.

## ARE DREAMS IMPORTANT?

Having dreams can be extremely healthy. Most of us who are healthy have dreams. The doctors who have treated me over the years are divided. One group has decided that I cannot dream, and the other group says that everyone dreams, and I merely cannot remember my dreams. If it is not going to decrease or affect the time I am to live, whether I dream seems to be a rather moot question. I have never met another person who cannot dream, and I have to say that while I cannot literally dream, I can "dream" just as much as any able-bodied person I have ever met.

I do not remember ever being able to dream and can recall how fascinated I was when I was told that normal people can see images when they sleep. No, I cannot ever imagine being able to dream, but I can hope for some things with as much energy and prayers as anyone. At the same time, I can be as dedicated to helping some things become reality as much as anyone I have ever met.

I say this because I have met other disabled people who were convinced that they could not accomplish what an able-bodied person could do simply because they could not do it themselves. Strangely enough, the effort that they convinced themselves they could not perform usually had nothing to do with their disability, but they had such low self-images that they would use any reason to convince themselves that they were less able and less worthy, often so they did not have to try.

It would be nice if I could say that nobody is foolish enough to decide to try to do something that he does not have the physical ability to accomplish. This goes just as much for the able-bodied person as a disabled person, and of course, the person who decides to attempt the effort that he is physically unable to accomplish for reasons that is beyond his or her control could be nuts. (Being desperate does not have to mean that a person is nuts.)

On the other hand, I have met disabled individuals who were fantastic at finding ways to accomplish some efforts that other people simply could not figure out. Once they decided to accomplish something, they continued until they were finished, and if it was something they could not accomplish in the standard way, they did what they had done for years: they figured out alternative methods. Able-bodied or disabled, this is what winners do. They make plans to accomplish some things and try until they accomplish them. The smartest people know that the best way to accomplish something is to ask for advice or help from experts. They are also smart enough to know what advice is appropriate and what is not. Winners are the people who find ways to solve problems that many other people are willing to let someone else do. Winners make the effort, do their very best, and accomplish what they need to accomplish.

## WHAT DOES PERSEVERING HAVE TO DO WITH SUCCESS?

There was a time when money was more available and businesses in the United States and business leaders would expect employees to transfer responsibilities they could not perform. Mistakes were something that somebody else could correct. Those days might be gone forever. For reasons that seem to be more complicated than I have the knowledge to completely understand, American businesses no longer have the money and the desire to hire people who have records that are less than perfect.

I can remember days from less than a decade ago, when people would go from job to job with little fear of being able to find another job; today, people who are leaving one job without another waiting might possibly never work again. Others who have lost jobs might realize that they may never work again, at least full time. I have read book after book that stresses the importance of determination and doing what one is being paid to do. Being told that you should do something without being told why means little or nothing to most people. But if you do not have the trait that compels you to want to do your best, you may find yourself out of a job one day soon.

But let's assume that you realize that your employment is determined by your perseverance and determination to do your job no matter what complications you may face. Employees are generally well trained to do whatever they are hired to do. People fortunate enough to be hired know what they must do to maintain their jobs. The rest of this chapter tells you what the winners need to do to stand out. Some people with jobs have no desire to make themselves more visible than necessary. The winners stand out because they are willing to do what they need to do to accomplish their goals, while others merely stand by. These winners, disabled or able-bodied, become the bosses.

## THE HIGHEST STANDARDS

Employees who are most likely to set high standards for themselves are the people who are trained to do this, and who realize what goals are reasonable and doable. This does not mean they have always been winners; most winners have learned to be winners by taking challenges and making them productive experiences. They do not brag about these successes but use what they do as examples of times or actions that led themselves and others to success. They create a picture. Most employers are grateful for this.

Anyone who's been around company managers and other executives has heard them brag about employees that stand out from their fellow employees. The usual purpose in awarding employees who accomplish admirable success is to encourage other leaders to produce employees that are also winners and who, in turn, compete with other employees. A true winner is not self-centered and only concerned with his own accomplishments. This type of person realizes that his efforts are part of the group efforts and is willing, even excited, to offer whatever help he can. He is a willing team member who does the best he can and recognizes the accomplishments of others. He is not embarrassed when rewarded for success and knows that the best leaders lead by example. He is motivated by high standards and expects others to be no different.

## TEAM PLAYERS

Winners are more than workers who accomplish outstanding things. They seem to know instantly that a positive attitude backed by appropriate preparation makes it possible to accomplish goals and make miracles. Winners set high standards that are doable and realize that positive presentations are what motivate others to do the same. They recognize the problems that might exist and motivate and help coworkers to find solutions. They realize that simply stressing problems does not accomplish the positive outcome the company expects, and they stress creating doable solutions.

## BEING AVERAGE

I have spent most of my life trying to be like other people, good enough that I would be the type of person that people would want to talk to. First off, there is nothing wrong with being average, and no one should ever be ashamed of being average. Who is the person to whom I gave the power to decide what is a standard for what is above or below 50 percent of the world's population? I have met people who have been intimidated by some people but who have gifts that are equally as important

I am rated 100 percent disabled by the Veterans Administration and the Social Security Administration. I am blessed because I cannot remember what I was like before my helicopter crash in Vietnam, and regardless of whether I can remember my past, my being alive has caused me to realize that this is a gift from God, for there are enough un-average things about me that I should be dead.

Over the years, I have met more people than I have bothered to count who allowed themselves to be victimized by someone's idea that they were not average, which is easy to define and impossible to give a non-wavering example of. I have met as many people who have used their disabilities as proof they are not average, while the truth is that I have never met the average person. In a world of about seven billion people, no two of us are exactly alike, and trying to decide what the average human being has to be like is like playing a computer game and is much less sensible. Here we go again, on the other hand, the trick comment that a winner has no desire to be average is the same as saying nothing. The super achiever is an average person who has achieved more things than most people or anyone else in a certain group of people, doing a specific task in the eyes of a specific group of leaders.

The people we choose to label winners are usually the best at something and have developed the ability to be one of the best more often than most people have. This above averageness, if there is such a term, is something that is learned, so there is no reason that everyone can't be a winner. If this is true, it is also a reality that we are all winners who have as equal an opportunity as the next person to learn and do fantastic things.

Winners are average people who developed the insight to be able to recognize when there is a cheaper and more efficient way to produce something, who feel they have found a better way to accomplish something, and who make the effort to share their insights with people who make a difference. Where some see a new idea as negative, the winner studies all the options possible and decides what is the most realistic and profitable change. He works with all the energy he has to create the reality he envisions and, when this moment or these moments come, he does not need anyone else to tell him. He changes his world and helps the world be a better place. This is what winners do. They change their part of the world in ways that make positive differences and are willing to do what it takes to accomplish goals.

Being average certainly is not a sin, but the achiever is not satisfied with being average and is not afraid to try to be more. This person continually strives for more and questions how he can do better.

## STRIVING TO ALWAYS DO BETTER

Winners can admit they have done some things that they are proud of, but they are never completely satisfied and continually strive to do better. Then they review what they have done to see if a new effort would be more productive than the old. If the changes do create improvements, they will be instituted. If the changes do not produce improved outcomes, they usually start searching for new ways to initiate improvements or study newer ideas.

Winners take risks when research indicates that the possibility for success is good enough to warrant the effort. They don't take foolish chances and respond to the possibility of success. When they face possible failures, they determine what they did that might have caused failure, and then they move on. They do not take any setback as a personal defeat, instead and they take what they know, learn more, apply what they know to what they have done before, make changes that seem appropriate, and try again. They do this until they are successful. In other words, they are willing to do what they need to do until they accomplish their goals

They believe in themselves and know that they have the mental assets to accomplish any goals they want to make reality. They accomplish everything humbly, and they are grateful for all their blessings. I did not write this book because I think I am one iota smarter than anyone else. On the other hand, as a mental health counselor, I have been blessed with so many good people who have wanted to share their issues with me and have invited me to help them find solutions to their problems.

Some people have trouble with the idea of making new friends. They seem to feel that making new friends naturally means abandoning old friends. In some ways, this could be considered a natural process. We all change as we mature. Our primary interests may change, and what once gave us great enjoyment may be exchanged for something new and different.

As we gain new experiences, we often begin to associate with people who are interested in the same things we are. When we have a question, we turn to these people for answers, and we continue to approach these people to exchange ideas that we feel are working in our lives. This is a natural evolution of a process that helps people grow and potentially be better and better people. This is what winners do. They make an earnest effort to associate with other people who want to be successful, people with similar dreams and values that include a desire to help other people be the most they can be.

Associate with experts in an attempt to learn from these people. You can give no greater compliment to someone than attempting to learn from him. This also increases the number of people you can turn to when you need help. It should never be the primary reason for making a friend, but it certainly does not hurt when the person you turn to for help is also a friend.

I have never stopped needing the circle of friends that I have developed over the years, and I feel that people who are unwilling to create a group of friends are missing so very much. I have accomplished some things in my life that I am proud of, but I've also known that my friends were my greatest motivators. They were the people who let me know whether a risk might be beyond my ability to overcome, and they were the people who applauded me for my success, showing more energy than anyone else. They were the people who helped me try to be the best, and that could be when I needed them the most. I make new friends whom I pray will always be friends. I do not remember my youth, but my friend Chris Seva, a retired airline pilot, and I were on the European Champion Babe Ruth baseball team in 1962. He flew the "big ones."

# Appendix 1

Reprinted with permission from Reader's Digest.

side of his head was indented from loss of bone and showed two burr holes where Army surgeons in South Vietnam had drilled exploratively. His weight had plunged from 145 pounds to an emaciated 80.

To Kathy, it seemed impossible that this pathetic figure was her husband. Only 16 weeks earlier, he had been in perfect health—and eager to reach Vietnam. The son of a career sergeant-major in the Army, he had enlisted after a year at the University of Oregon, where he had been a brilliant student and president of the freshman honor society.

"I can't go on with school while men are dying out there," he had told Kathy in their frequent talks about the war. "I've got to do something to save lives, and the best way is for me to become a helicopter pilot."

Jim and Kathy were married shortly before he went to South Vietnam, where he immediately saw combat. He flew day and night, and in less than four months was shot down three times. On the third crash he drifted his falling ship into trees at an angle that exposed himself to the greatest danger and his three crewmen to the least. At impact, the broken but still-spinning rotor blades smashed through the cockpit, tore his helmet to bits, gouged out part of his skull and battered his brain. He was the only one injured.

**Trapped Animal.** Fifteen days after the crash Jim was wheeled into Madigan General, where a medical team headed by Maj. George Palmer (not his real name) quickly went to work. They made repairs on his battered body, fed him nutrients intravenously, got his blood chemistry into balance. But they could do nothing about the brain damage that caused his strange coma. After a few days his eyes opened, but they remained unfocused and expressionless. Frenetically active, he had to be tied to the bed with towels. Incomprehensible animal sounds came from his throat.

Kathy and Jim's mother were at his bedside throughout the day, trying to break through the coma by giving him every possible expression of love. Periodically, they removed his arm restraints. And each time he tried to throw himself out of bed, biting, snarling, growling. Unable to express himself like a human being, he behaved like a trapped animal.

Major Palmer could offer no hope. "We were losing him," he recalls, "and I had the feeling that he wanted to go. He had been so cruelly hurt that life was unbearable."

Jim's mother, a surgery-room nurse in a civilian hospital, also recognized that her son was sinking. "You and I know that he is dying," she told Major Palmer. "Can't you try something else?"

The major had concluded that Jim remained alive only because of the loving attention of his wife and mother. What might help to lift the coma, he thought, would be the additional care and concern of others.

*Drama in Real Life: The Long Return of Warrant Officer Meade.*

side of his head was indented from loss of bone and showed two burr holes where Army surgeons in South Vietnam had drilled exploratively. His weight had plunged from 145 pounds to an emaciated 80.

To Kathy, it seemed impossible that this pathetic figure was her husband. Only 16 weeks earlier, he had been in perfect health—and eager to reach Vietnam. The son of a career sergeant-major in the Army, he had enlisted after a year at the University of Oregon, where he had been a brilliant student and president of the freshman honor society.

"I can't go on with school while men are dying out there," he had told Kathy in their frequent talks about the war. "I've got to do something to save lives, and the best way is for me to become a helicopter pilot."

Jim and Kathy were married shortly before he went to South Vietnam, where he immediately saw combat. He flew day and night, and in less than four months was shot down three times. On the third crash he drifted his falling ship into trees at an angle that exposed himself to the greatest danger and his three crewmen to the least. At impact, the broken but still-spinning rotor blades smashed through the cockpit, tore his helmet to bits, gouged out part of his skull and battered his brain. He was the only one injured.

**Trapped Animal.** Fifteen days after the crash Jim was wheeled into Madigan General, where a medical team headed by Maj. George Palmer (not his real name) quickly went to work. They made repairs on his battered body, fed him nutrients intravenously, got his blood chemistry into balance. But they could do nothing about the brain damage that caused his strange coma. After a few days his eyes opened, but they remained unfocused and expressionless. Frenetically active, he had to be tied to the bed with towels. Incomprehensible animal sounds came from his throat.

Kathy and Jim's mother were at his bedside throughout the day, trying to break through the coma by giving him every possible expression of love. Periodically, they removed his arm restraints. And each time he tried to throw himself out of bed, biting, snarling, growling. Unable to express himself like a human being, he behaved like a trapped animal.

Major Palmer could offer no hope. "We were losing him," he recalls, "and I had the feeling that he wanted to go. He had been so cruelly hurt that life was unbearable."

Jim's mother, a surgery-room nurse in a civilian hospital, also recognized that her son was sinking. "You and I know that he is dying," she told Major Palmer. "Can't you try something else?"

The major had concluded that Jim remained alive only because of the loving attention of his wife and mother. What might help to lift the coma, he thought, would be the additional care and concern of others.

Perhaps the answer could be found in the hospital's orthopedic Ward 13, which housed some of the Vietnam war's most seriously disabled amputees.

"Ward 13 had a fine spirit," Major Palmer later explained. "The men there, having fought depression and emotional withdrawal, were more capable of helping Jim than all the hospital's doctors and nurses. Ward 13 was his only chance, although a remote one."

**"Help Us."** First Lt. Carole Burke, head nurse on the ward, told its occupants only that a young chopper pilot with a head injury, who could neither talk nor respond, was being admitted. She asked nothing of them. She knew they had a great respect for these pilots; each, in fact, had been carried from the battlefield to a hospital by Army helicopter.

The men glanced up casually as Jim was wheeled into the ward. Two nurses removed the towel restraints from his raw wrists, then posted themselves on either side of his bed. In a few minutes a patient in a cast hobbled over. "I'll stay with him," he said. Soon two other patients drifted by and began a conversation; although Jim seemed oblivious to it, he was included. During the next 24 hours the men lounged around Jim's bed, spoon-fed him meals, played the radio, bantered, kidded with the nurses. All the while Jim was treated as if he were "there"—aware, participating.

After a few days, Jim's hyperactivity—the biting and writhing—

subsided. He took long naps, curled like a fetus. It may have been that he was preparing to be "born" again, Major Palmer surmised, as hitherto unused cells in the right side of the brain were being activated to take over the functions of the destroyed cells in the left side.

When he grew restless in bed, nurses and patients moved him into a wheelchair and pushed him into the semicircle of amputees around the television set. "Want to watch a ball game, Jim?" one asked. No response. "Want some ice cream, Jim?" No response.

One day, when Nurse Burke was helping him into a wheelchair, Jim swung his forearm sharply against her head. It seemed a deliberate movement, perhaps to express impatience. "Jim," she said, "we're trying to understand you. Help us." No response.

**"I—Love—You."** More than a month went by while the men eagerly watched Jim for any sign of change. Then one day a veteran told Nurse Burke, "I think he looked at me. For just a flash."

Gradually Jim's eyes began to focus, to look at things, at people. And now, as he began emerging from his coma, puzzlement replaced the empty, unseeing expression. Neither he nor the doctors realized at this time that the chopper blades had destroyed a portion of his brain's memory cells. Like an infant, Jim was looking at a world he couldn't recognize.

Actually, he was more helpless

than an infant. He couldn't talk, laugh or cry. The pain in his left leg was deep and searing, but he had no way to express it. As the days passed, and a part of his intelligence returned, he became convinced that his inability to communicate meant he was dying. He sank into deep depression.

But Ward 13 would have none of it. Prodding, cajoling, they forced him into action. He learned to nod or shake his head in answer to questions. He learned to eat on his own power—by reaching erratically for the food and throwing it toward his mouth. He wanted to talk. He worked his mouth, grimaced, pushed, fought. But the words simply wouldn't come out.

Then, early one Monday, it happened. Nurse Burke entered Ward 13 with a cheery "Good morning, gentlemen." As she passed Jim's wheelchair she thought she heard him answer, "Goo' moorn'." Was it wishful hearing? His eyes told her that he *had* made the sounds.

That same day, he greeted Kathy with three barely understandable and obviously rehearsed words. "I —love—you," he said.

Her heart jumped. She repeated the words to him. Then she pointed to her expanding middle. "Baby," she said. He tried furiously to say the word. He couldn't. He tried other words. They wouldn't come. Then he went limp, as if to say, "Why try? It's hopeless."

Kathy leaned over him. "You can't give up," she whispered. "We need

you. You're going to make it." Then she excused herself, went to the ladies' room and bawled, out of hope and fear, and sympathy for her husband in his terrible struggle.

**Making It.** Nothing came easy to Jim as he fought to "grow up." To read, he first had to relearn his ABCs. Then he progressed to children's books of the "Look, Jane, there's Spot" variety. His greatest problem was making his legs, hands and voice respond to his brain's commands. It took him nearly a year to go from scattering food across the table to cutting his meat and bringing it accurately to his mouth.

Writing, even simple words like "cat," was an ordeal. He would forget how to spell the word or how to print the letters. He couldn't write in a straight line, make the letters the same size or keep one from overlapping another. But, finally, there it was—a legible C A T.

It took Jim nearly three years of sweat, strain and determination to walk without supports. From a wheelchair, and still wearing a leg cast, he moved to crutches. One afternoon he joined other disabled veterans who were bouncing a ball off a handball wall. He dropped his crutches to see if he could maintain balance and move just a little. He reached for the ball—and fell. Choking back tears of frustration, he picked up his crutches, went around to the back of the gym and pounded his head against the wall.

His father understood his feelings. "Jim," he told him, "you've

James P. Meade, Jr., Ph.D.

done a lot of things that most people thought you'd never be able to do. I know you can learn to walk. Let's get to work on it." At his father's home, where Jim now spent periodic leaves, the elder Meade built a 30-foot-long wood platform with hip-high parallel railings. Using the railings for support, Jim tried to walk. He fell, got up, fell —and kept falling until, exhausted, he could no longer pull himself up.

Undaunted, he crawled up and down the platform, trying to coördinate the movements of his legs and arms. He performed these exercises for weeks until he could crawl as well as a normal year-old infant. Back to the rails, now, and he was able to take some steps without falling. "I've got to make it," he told himself. "I've got to." And his father, beside him every minute, assured him, "You will, you will."

From the parallel bars he went to canes, walking, weaving, staggering, falling. Slowly, over the months, he learned to maintain his balance, to walk in a straight line, to maneuver street curbs. In February 1970 he walked into Ward 13 with a big grin on his face—and no canes. Thirty months after one authority had labeled him a "hopeless vegetable," Jim Meade was clearly making it.

**From D to B.** In September 1969 he had taken another long step, en-rolling in the two-year Mt. Hood Community College on the outskirts of Portland. It was tough. He was self-conscious about his limping gait and occasionally slurred speech. He couldn't take notes fast enough. Homework took him three times longer than the average student.

"I felt so dumb, so worthless," Jim recalls. "Why, I even had to learn to add, subtract and multiply. It was terrible not to be able to keep up."

He became despondent. "Then he remembered what people had done for him," recalls his college counselor, psychologist Patrick Loughary. "He developed an ambition to help others, as he had been helped. His determination returned, and he changed remarkably. In eight months he rose from a D to a B student."

Jim received his diploma from Mt. Hood in June 1970 and is now studying for a degree in psychology at Portland State University. "I want to get into work where I can use what I've learned to help people," Jim explains. "A person who is deeply hurt feels very lonely. It's hard to survive this feeling. But love can make the difference. Even in my coma I must have felt the love of my family and ward mates, and felt my love for them. If I hadn't, there would have been no reason to go on. Surely, I would have died."

*Urban Scrawl.* A neighborhood fence chalked with the usual vulgarities and an occasional "John Loves Mary" offers one reassuring bit of graffiti: "Ma Loves Pa."    —Contributed by Arthur J. Moody

# Appendix 2

**Vietnam Helicopter Pilots Association**

*devoted to the helicopter pilots who served their country*
*in Southeast Asia during the Vietnam era*
*hereby proclaims that*

## James P. Meade, Jr.

*has been granted all privileges in accordance*
*with the Constitution and By Laws of this organization*

*as a* General Member

**1194**
Member Number

Executive Director                President

*Vietnam Helicopter Pilots Association*

The Board of Directors
of the

**California State Psychological Association**

takes pleasure in announcing that

*James P. Meade, Jr., Ph.D.*

having fulfilled all the requirements, is hereby entitled
to the rights and privileges of Membership
in the Association.

President

Membership Chairman

To advance Psychology as a science, a profession & as a means of promoting human welfare

*Board of Directors, California State Psychological Association.*

# The President of the United States of America

*presents this certificate for*

## Outstanding Community Achievement

*of*

## Vietnam Era Veterans

*to*

### James P. Meade, Jr.

*In recognition of service to the Nation in time of war and outstanding community achievement in time of peace. Presented as part of the national observance of Vietnam Veterans Week, May 28 through June 3, 1979.*

*Jimmy Carter*

The White House
Washington, D.C.

*Daniel K. White*

*Outstanding Achievement of Vietnam Veterans,*
*June 3, 1979, from President Jimmy Carter.*

# The University of the South
## School of Theology

To all who have been baptized
into the ministry of Christ's Church:
We take pleasure in commending to you

# James P. Meade Jr.

who has completed the program of
Theological Education by Extension
Education for Ministry
as provided and administered by the
School of Theology, the University of the South

Sunday, May 30, 2004

*Edward O. de Bary*
PROGRAM DIRECTOR

*Joel Cunningham*
VICE CHANCELLOR
THE UNIVERSITY OF THE SOUTH

*University of the South School of Theology, May 30, 2004.*

**SAN DIEGO COUNTY BOARD OF SUPERVISORS**
LEON L. WILLIAMS, VICE CHAIRMAN

NATIONAL & STATE BOARDS

NATIONAL ASSOCIATION OF
COUNTIES

COUNTY SUPERVISORS ASSOCIATION
OF CALIFORNIA

SOUTHERN CALIFORNIA HAZARDOUS
WASTE MANAGEMENT AUTHORITY

REGIONAL BOARDS

METROPOLITAN TRANSIT
DEVELOPMENT BOARD

SAN DIEGO WATER AUTHORITY
WATER RECLAMATION
ADVISORY COMMITTEE

REGIONAL TASK FORCE
ON THE HOMELESS

CITY/COUNTY REINVESTMENT
TASK FORCE

PRIVATE INDUSTRY COUNCIL
REGIONAL EMPLOYMENT
TRAINING CONSORTIUM
POLICY BOARD

SERVICE AUTHORITY FOR
FREEWAY EMERGENCIES

July 25, 1989

James P. Meade, Ph.D.
850 State Street, No. 412
San Diego, CA  92101

Dear Dr. Meade:

It is with sincere regret that I accept your resignation as Chairman of the Self Esteem Task Force, however, I do understand your need to increase avenues available to Veterans.  Therefore, I commend your efforts to create a Vietnam Veterans of America Chapter in San Diego.

Such a chapter is no doubt needed and thereby a welcome addition to our community as your chapter grows in size and stature, I look forward to cooperative efforts between the Self Esteem Task Force's Veterans Committee and your Vietnam Vets of America Chapter.

Sincerely,

Leon L. Williams
Supervisor

1600 PACIFIC HIGHWAY • SAN DIEGO, CALIFORNIA 92101 • (619) 531-5544

*San Diego Board of Supervisors, Leon L. Williams, July 25, 1989.*

THE WHITE HOUSE

WASHINGTON

August 1, 1989

Dear Dr. Meade:

On behalf of the President, thank you for taking the time to write.

The President has said, "From now on in America, any definition of a successful life must include serving others." I see your efforts and the efforts of your organization as embodying this idea. Your success has purpose and as a result you have enriched the lives of many. I applaud your endeavors.

National service is the initiative of individuals who see a need and then act to fill it. Working together, individuals and business possess the means to solve many of our nation's problems.

However, possessing the resources is only part of the solution. As Americans we must understand that we possess the responsibility to help one another. Yours is a shining example that individuals and organizations alike accept that responsibility.

The task you have undertaken is not an easy one. But, through your determination, ingenuity, and hard work you are making a difference. Good luck.

Sincerely,

C. Gregg Petersmeyer
Deputy Assistant to the President
and Director, Office of National Service

Dr. James P. Meade, Jr.
President
Vietnam Veterans of America
Suite 108
850 State Street
San Diego, CA 92101

*Letter from the White House, August 1, 1989.*

# THE UNITED STATES OF AMERICA

TO ALL WHO SHALL SEE THESE PRESENTS, GREETING:

THIS IS TO CERTIFY THAT
THE PRESIDENT OF THE UNITED STATES OF AMERICA
HAS AWARDED THE

## PURPLE HEART

ESTABLISHED BY GENERAL GEORGE WASHINGTON
AT NEWBURGH, NEW YORK, AUGUST 7, 1782
TO

FOR WOUNDS RECEIVED
IN ACTION

GIVEN UNDER MY HAND IN THE CITY OF WASHINGTON
THIS          DAY OF           1967

*Purple Heart from April 27, 1967, on May 20, 1967.*

169

December 20, 1989

Mr. Jim Meade
850 State Street #108
San Diego, CA  92101

Dear Jim,

Congratulations again on the success of your "Unsolved Mysteries" segment. The most satisfying part of our job is bringing people together when a story is solved.

The episode containing your story was one of our highest rated of the season. The Neilson numbers were a 19.2 rating and a 32 share. Each rating point stands for nearly a million homes. If you figure that between two and three people are watching in each home, that comes to between forty and sixty million viewers. Quite an audience!

Thank you again for opening your heart to us on "Unsolved Mysteries". All of us here wish you continued happiness and success.

Best Regards,

Stuart Schwartz
COORDINATING PRODUCER

/ss

COSGROVE/MEURER PRODUCTIONS, INC.
4303 West Verdugo Avenue, Burbank, California 91505  Tel: (818) 843-5600  Fax: (818) 843-8585

*Letter from Unsolved Mysteries, December 20, 1989.*

**FRESNO AMERICAN INDIAN COUNCIL, INC.**

SUITE 10 · 2ND FLOOR, 20 NORTH DEWITT, CLOVIS, CALIFORNIA 93612
ADMINISTRATION                         MANPOWER, SENIOR, & SOCIAL SERVICES
209-297-1349                           209-297-7885

March 20, 1985

To whom it may concern:

The Fresno Amreican Indian Council would like to introduce
Dr. James Meade, Counselor, Fresno Vet. Center.  Dr. Meade
is working in corporation with the Fresno American Indian
Council to provide Service and Assistance to Indian Veterans
in the Fresno-Madera areas.

Your time given to Dr. Meade is appreciated by Fresno
American Indian Council.  If you have any questions or if
we can be of assistance please feel free to contact me at
209/297-7885 or at our offices at 20 N. DeWitt Ave, Suite 10,
Clovis, California 93612.

Sincerely,

R. Roger Ince,
Executive Director

RRI/bh

*Letter from the Fresno American Indian Council, March 20, 1985.*

**Robert Schuller**

Crystal Cathedral

May 30, 1990

Dr. James Meade
350 State Street #105?
San Diego, CA 92101

Dear Jim,

How wonderful to have you here! Thank you so much! You were great! I am so grateful for individuals like you who are willing to share their positive faith with the entire world!

We are proud to be the world's first global church. We are proud to include you in the crusade to bring Christ's message of peace, hope and love to a hurting world. I am proud to be your friend!

God loves you and so do I!

*Robert H. Schuller*

Robert H. Schuller

(Dictated by Dr. Schuller and
signed in his absence)

RHS:bt

12141 Lewis Street, Garden Grove, California 92840

*Letter from Robert Schuller, May 30, 1990.*

172

*The Vietnam War, series conducted by James Meade, Jr., at Mesa College in California.*

## SHARP
### MEMORIAL HOSPITAL

atient Brain Injury Services
RP REHABILITATION CENTER
vision of Sharp Memorial Hospital

ATTENTION ALL DAY TREATMENT AND DAY HEALTH PARTICIPANTS AND

FAMILY MEMBERS AND FRIENDS OF THE PROGRAMS

On February 28 at 6:00 PM, we have a distinguished guest speaker,
Dr. James Meade, scheduled to talk to brain injury survivors and
their friends and families. Dr. Meade incurred a serious head
injury on May 8, 1967 when his helicopter was shot down in
Vietnam. He is an excellent speaker and has an exceptional
ability to articulate the challenges and difficulties experienced
by brain injured individuals and their loved ones. Please come
for an inspirational, motivational and supportive presentation by
an individual who has experienced the arduous task of
rehabilitation, and is committed to helping his "brothers and
sisters", as they too struggle with recovery from brain injury.

Please reserve a seat by calling Cindy Wood at 541-4415 by
February 27, 1989.

Presentation will take place at Sharp Outpatient Brain Injury
Services, 3665 Ruffin Road, Suite 120, San Diego, CA   92123.
Don't miss this presentation, guaranteed to warm your heart and
give you motivation to keep on working towards your goals.

## ABOUT JAMES MEADE, Ph.D.

James Meade is a clinical psychologist who also has a master of arts in counseling. He has provided counseling to both able-bodied and disabled people, older adults and families.

He is the author of *Making Reality: Coping With Limitations Successfully*, published by Carlton Press of New York in 1981.

Since 1986, James has been in private practice. He worked as a Veteran's Administration outreach therapist from 1984 to 1986.

From 1974 to 1983, James was a sales representative for Hunt-Wesson Foods.

## FROM NEAR FATAL COMBAT WOUNDS TO GRADUATION WITH HONORS

As an Army Warrant Officer during the Viet Nam war, he was awarded the Distinguished Flying Cross, the Bronze Star, two Purple Hearts, ten Air Medals, and other commendations. His helicopter was shot down three times during three months of combat. This certainly qualifies for active duty experience for a young man who was commissioned at the age of 19.

When his helicopter was shot down on May 8, 1967, he received the wounds he is still recovering from.

James Meade was presented with the Outstanding Community Achievement certificate of Vietnam Era Veterans from President Jimmy Carter in 1979 for his

*Sharpe Memorial Hospital, lecture by James Meade, Jr., PhD, February 28, 1989.*

"Involuntary Foster Workers"?

✝

# Crystal Cathedral Ministries

Hour of Power • 13280 Chapman Avenue • Garden Grove, CA 92640

September 4, 1990

Dr. James Meade
850 State Street #108
San Diego, CA  92101

Dear Dr. Meade:

As a tribute to our troops in the Middle East, the
Hour of Power is proud to re-air our special
celebration of freedom, taped on Memorial Day Sunday.

It is our prayer that the families and loved ones of
the men and women of the Armed Forces will find the
inspiration and comfort they need to make it through
these challenging times.

This special patriotic program will be airing on the
Hour of Power, Sunday, September 9, 1990 throughout
the United States of America.

Thank you for participating in our special ministry.
God loves you and so do we!

Sincerely,

*Arvella Schuller*

Arvella Schuller

(Dictated by Mrs. Schuller
 and signed in her absence)

AS/sm
Enclosure

*Letter, second invitation for Hour of Power, September 4, 1990.*

**Six who served:** Sens. Robert Kerry, D-Neb. (foreground left); Max Cleland, D-Ga. (foreground center); John Kerry, D-Mass. (foreground right); John McCain, R-Ariz. (background left); Chuck Hagel, R-Neb. (background center); and Chuck Robb, D-Va., participate Friday in a ceremony on the 15th anniversary of the Vietnam Veterans Memorial.

**MAX CLELAND**
SECRETARY OF STATE

James --

you are truly incredible! God bless your efforts in your travels abroad! Let me know if I can ever help! Love ya, brother!

*Picture and note from Max Cleland and other senators.*

**JIM BATES**
44th DISTRICT, CALIFORNIA

COMMITTEE ON ENERGY
AND COMMERCE

COMMITTEE ON
GOVERNMENT OPERATIONS

COMMITTEE ON HOUSE
ADMINISTRATION

CHAIRMAN
SUBCOMMITTEE ON
PROCUREMENT AND PRINTING

## Congress of the United States
### House of Representatives

PLEASE REPLY TO:

224 CANNON BUILDING
WASHINGTON, D.C. 20515
(202) 225-5452

MARKETPLACE AT THE GROVE
3450 COLLEGE AVENUE, #220
SAN DIEGO, CA 92115
(619) 287-8851

430 DAVIDSON STREET, SUITE A
CHULA VISTA, CA 92010
(619) 691-1166

February 26, 1990

Dr. James Meade
850 State Street, #108
San Diego, CA  92101

Dear James:

Thank you for the advice you have given me as a member of the
Disability Advisory Subcommittee.  I hope that you will continue
to meet with me and share your concerns on some of the issues
facing individuals with disability today.

I have scheduled our next meeting for March 2, 1990 from 5:00 to
6:00 p.m. in my office which is located at 3450 College Avenue,
Marketplace at the Grove, suite #220, San Diego.

The next agenda will include a discussion on Bill's HR71 and HR2273
and HR2863, and other related legislation pending before the 101st
Congress.

Please contact Jeralene Taylor at (619) 691-1166 to confirm your
attendance or if you have any questions. Thank you for your
participation in this very important process.  I am looking forward
to meeting with you on March 2nd.

Sincerely,

JIM BATES
Member of Congress

Enclosure

JB:jt

*Letter from Jim Bates, February 26, 1990.*

## The California Community Colleges

JAMES P. MEADE, JR.

The Board of Governors of the California Community Colleges, acting in accordance with the authority vested in it, certifies that the person named above has satisfied the educational and occupational requirements for the following credential

COMMUNITY COLLEGE INSTRUCTOR CREDENTIAL

This certificate authorizes the holder to perform the services specified on the reverse of this document subject to the limitations specified thereon.

Subject Matter Area: Psychology

PRESIDENT, BOARD OF GOVERNORS
California Community Colleges

Issued: June 27, 1984    Valid for life

CHANCELLOR
California Community Colleges

*California Community College instructor credentials, June 27, 1984.*